### *About the Author*

Born in Germany, Edgar Rothermich studied music and sound engin[...] prestigious Tonmeister program at the Berlin Institute of Technology [...] University of Arts (UdK) in Berlin where he graduated in 1989 with a Master's Degree. He worked as a composer and music producer in Berlin, and moved to Los Angeles in 1991 where he continued his work on numerous projects in the music and film industry ("The Celestine Prophecy", "Outer Limits", "Babylon 5", "What the Bleep Do We Know", "Fuel", "Big Money Rustlas").

For over 20 years, Edgar has had a successful musical partnership with electronic music pioneer and founding Tangerine Dream member Christopher Franke. In addition to his collaboration with Christopher, Edgar has been working with other artists, as well as on his own projects.

In 2010 he started to release his solo records in the "Why Not …" series with different styles and genres. The current releases are "Why Not Solo Piano", "Why Not Electronica", "Why Not Electronica Again", and "Why Not 90s Electronica". This previously unreleased album was produced in 1991/1992 by Christopher Franke. All albums are available on Amazon and iTunes, including the 2012 release, the re-recording of the Blade Runner Soundtrack.

In addition to composing music, Edgar Rothermich is writing technical manuals with a unique style, focusing on rich graphics and diagrams to explain concepts and functionality of software applications under his popular GEM series (Graphically Enhanced Manuals). His best-selling titles are available as printed books on Amazon, as Multi-Touch eBooks on the iBooks Store, and as pdf downloads from his website.

Since 2017, Edgar Rothermich is Adjunct Professor at the Fullerton College Fine Arts Department.

www.DingDingMusic.com                    GEM@DingDingMusic.com

 ### *Special Thanks*

Special thanks to my beautiful wife, Li, for her love, support, and understanding during those long hours of working on the books. And not to forget my son, Winston. Waiting for him during soccer practice or Chinese class always gives me extra time to work on a few chapters.

The manual is based on Logic Pro X v10.3.2

Manual: Print Version 2017-0719

ISBN-13: 978-1973784609

ISBN-10: 1973784602

### *About the GEM (Graphically Enhanced Manuals)*

> ## UNDERSTAND, not just LEARN
>
> What are Graphically Enhanced Manuals? They're a new type of manual with a visual approach that helps you UNDERSTAND a program, not just LEARN it. No need to read through 500 pages of dry text explanations. Rich graphics and diagrams help you to get that "aha" effect and make it easy to comprehend difficult concepts. The Graphically Enhanced Manuals help you master a program much faster with a much deeper understanding of concepts, features, and workflows in a very intuitive way that is easy to understand.

All titles are available in three different formats:

........... pdf downloads from my website www.DingDingMusic.com/Manuals

............ multi-touch iBooks on Apple's iBooks Store

.... printed books on Amazon.com

(some manuals are also available in Deutsch, Español, 简体中文)

For a list of all the available titles and bundles: www.DingDingMusic.com/Manuals

To be notified about new releases and updates, subscribe to subscribe@DingDingMusic.com

 ### *About the Formatting*

I use a specific color code in my books:

*Green colored text* indicates keyboard shortcuts or mouse actions. I use the following abbreviations: **sh** (shift key), **ctr** (control key), **opt** (option key), **cmd** (command key). A plus (+) between the keys means that you have to press all those keys at the same time.

**sh+opt+K** means: Hold the shift and the option key while pressing the K key.

*(light green text in parenthesis indicates the name of the Key Command)*

*Brown colored text* indicates Menu Commands with a greater sign (➤) indicating submenus.

*Edit ➤ Source Media ➤ All* means "Click on the Edit Menu, scroll down to Source Media, and select the submenu All.

Blue arrows indicate what happens if you click on an item or popup menu ●━━━➤

Gray Text indicates important terminology.

# Table of Contents

**1 - Introduction** _____ **6**

*About This Book* ------------------------------------------------------ 6
  The Karma Approach ........................................................... 7

*The GEM Advantage* ------------------------------------------------------ 8

**2 - Overview** _____ **11**

*Highlights* ------------------------------------------------------------- 11

*Housekeeping* ----------------------------------------------------------- 12
  New/Updated Sounds ............................................................ 12
  Bug Fixes .................................................................. 13
  Improvements ............................................................... 13

**3 - New Big Features** _____ **14**

  GUI Redraw Speed Improvements ............................................... 14
  Modified Drummer Interface .................................................. 15
  New Drummer Genre - Percussion .............................................. 21
  Loop Browser Changes ........................................................ 34
  Yellow Apple Loops .......................................................... 37

**4 - Main Window** _____ **42**

*Toolbar* ----------------------------------------------------------------- 42
  Renamed Items in Toolbar Configuration Popover .............................. 42
  Use Capture Recording for Smart Controls ................................... 43

*Control Bar* ------------------------------------------------------------- 44
  Additional Display Modes .................................................... 44
  Cycle Button Moved Next to the Transport Controls .......................... 45
  "Recording Preferences..." Command in Record Button Shortcut Menu .......... 45

*Ruler* ------------------------------------------------------------------- 46
  Trimming/Moving Cycle Area doesn't cover Ruler Tracks anymore .............. 46

*Global Tracks* ----------------------------------------------------------- 46
  Visually Overlapping Infinite Marker Tracks ................................ 46

*Menu Bar* ---------------------------------------------------------------- 47
  Corrected Key Command for "Reset Individual Track Zoom" .................... 47

*Region Inspector* -------------------------------------------------------- 47
  Region Transpose value is displayed in the Region Header .................. 47
  New Transpose and Fine Tune Parameters ..................................... 48

*Track Header* ------------------------------------------------------------ 50
  Duplicate Track with Record Enable .......................................... 50
  Show/Hide Inactive Track Alternatives on All Tracks ........................ 50
  Menu Items for Track Header Component rearranged ........................... 51
  Updated Track Icons ......................................................... 52
  Drummer Character Name displayed with the Track Name ...................... 53
  Changes on Shortcut Menu for the Track Header ............................. 53

*Workspace* --------------------------------------------------------------- 54
  Vertical Crosshair Line for Loop Trimming .................................. 54
  Plus Button at the right border of Drummer Regions ........................ 54
  Plus Button Behavior ........................................................ 55
  Bounce In Place (BiP) Drummer Summing Stacks ............................... 55
  Bounce In Place (BiP) Drummer Summing Stacks ............................... 56

Trim Region Start/End to Previous/Next Region as Menu Commands .................56
Opt+drag Plugins in Selection-Based Processing Window.........................................57
Trimming the Start of an Alias MIDI Regions converts it to Real Copy..................57
Select Tracks on Region Selection ..........................................................................58
Renamed Fade Out Command......................................................................................58

## Track Alternatives ---------------------------------------------------------------------------------59
Rename Active Track Alternative .................................................................................59
Track Alternative Shortcut Menu ................................................................................59
Show/Hide Inactive Track Alternative on All Tracks................................................59

# 5 - Editors _____60

## Piano Roll Editor-------------------------------------------------------------------------------------60
Drums Names in Note Labels .......................................................................................60

## Event List ------------------------------------------------------------------------------------------------61
Mute Column displays "M" instead of a Dot ............................................................61
Display Meta Event Name in Info Column ................................................................61
"Increase/Decrease Last Clicked Parameter by 10" for MIDI Notes....................62

## Global Edits ---------------------------------------------------------------------------------------------62
New Key Command "Copy Section Between Locators (Global)" ..........................62

## Marker List ----------------------------------------------------------------------------------------------63
New Icons for Scene Markers in Lock Column..........................................................63
Select Markers with Cmd+Click................................................................................63

## Score Editor --------------------------------------------------------------------------------------------64
Display Markers in the Linear View Mode ................................................................64
Key Command "Toggle View" includes all Views....................................................64

## Flex Pitch ------------------------------------------------------------------------------------------------64
New "Reset All" Command............................................................................................64

# 6 - Mixer & Plugins _____65

## Mixer---------------------------------------------------------------------------------------------------------65
Audio Device Controls for Stereo Tracks ................................................................65
Solo-Safe remains on a solo/un-soloed Track........................................................65
Restrict Automatic Bus Assignment to higher Bus Numbers................................66
Drag Pan Position And Pan Spread on the Pan Control .......................................67
Output Selection on New Tracks Dialog displays Custom Labels.......................67

## Smart Controls -----------------------------------------------------------------------------------------68
Tuner Button on Smart Controls Window for Audio Tracks...................................68
Amp Designer and Pedalboard Button on Smart Controls Window....................68

## I/O -------------------------------------------------------------------------------------------------------------69
Bounce Dialog ...............................................................................................................69

## Plugins ----------------------------------------------------------------------------------------------------69
Linked Dual Mono Mode ("Couple").........................................................................69
Configuration Button now is the Gear Button ........................................................70
Bypass individual Plugin Channels (fixed)...............................................................70
Toggle "Recent Plugins" Functionality in Plugin Menu .........................................71
Shift+click to close all Plugin Windows....................................................................71
Correlation Meter Reaction Time ..............................................................................72
Surround Panner new GUI............................................................................................72

## Drummer --------------------------------------------------------------------------------------------------73
Only one Drummer Region as Default........................................................................73
Empty Drummer Editor..................................................................................................73
Switch between a Basic Kit and Producer Kit+........................................................74
New Drum Machine Designer (DMD) Behavior........................................................75

## Channel EQ-----------------------------------------------------------------------------------------------76
All EQ Handles are visible when hovering over the EQ Display.............................76

## Arpeggiator ----------------------------------------------------------------------------------------------76

      *Adjust the Length of individual Step*..............................................................76

   **Retro Synth** ------------------------------------------------------------------------------------------**77**
      *Additional fourth Modulation Slider*.............................................................77

   **Alchemy** -----------------------------------------------------------------------------------------------**78**
      *New Browser Column Options*......................................................................78
      *New Options for in the Note Properties Menu*.........................................78
      *New Synthesized Formant Filter Shapes*.................................................79
      *A new "Tune Control" in the Noise Section*............................................79
      *New Additive Effects*....................................................................................80
      *Effects are organized in Categories*........................................................80
      *New Default Rate for the Arpeggiator is 1/16*........................................81
      *New Key Trigger "Cycle Reset"*..................................................................81
      *21 New Arpeggiator Presets*.....................................................................81
      *Default Auto Gain in Morph XY/Lin is off*...............................................81
      *Default Keyswitch is now "KEYSW1"*........................................................82
      *Other Alchemy Improvements*...................................................................82

## 7 - Miscellaneous                                       83

   **More Flat Design** ------------------------------------------------------------------------------------**83**
      *Updated Project Chooser Dialog*..............................................................83
      *New Track Dialog*..........................................................................................84

   **Touch Bar** --------------------------------------------------------------------------------------------------**85**
      *Key Command access from any View*.......................................................85
      *More Images for Key Commands*...............................................................85
      *Two Lines for Long Key Command Name*..................................................85
      *Two Lines for Long Smart Controls Names*.............................................85

   **Environment** -----------------------------------------------------------------------------------------**86**
      *Environment Window again has a Link Button*.......................................86
      *Opt+click to Clear All Monitor Objects*....................................................86
      *MIDI Transformer with Note Scale Parameter*........................................87

   **More Changes** --------------------------------------------------------------------------------------**88**
      *New Yellow Quick Help Popovers*...............................................................88
      *Window Header of Transport Float is renamed to "Transport"* ...............90
      *Window Header has changed from "Strip Silence" to "Remove Silence"* ...........90
      *"Do not show this message again" checkbox in Add Tempo Dialog*.................91
      *"Don't show again" checkbox in Aux Import Dialog*.............................91
      *Disconnect/Reconnect Split Stereo Files*..............................................92
      *Final Cut Pro XML imports Parent Roles as Folder Stacks*...................93
      *Music XML Export to Dorico*.......................................................................94
      *Logic Remote Improvements*.....................................................................94

## 8 - Preferences - Project Settings - Menus               95

   **Preferences** ----------------------------------------------------------------------------------------------**95**
   **Project Settings** ----------------------------------------------------------------------------------**97**
   **Main Menu** ------------------------------------------------------------------------------------------------**97**

## 9 - Key Command Changes                               98

   **New - Renamed** ------------------------------------------------------------------------------------------**98**

## Conclusion                                              99

# 1 - Introduction

## About This Book

Logic Pro X v10.3.2 is considered a minor ".point" upgrade. However, besides the usual bug fixes and general improvements, it has quite a list of changes and additions plus some big new features.

 ### Official Release Notes

For a comprehensive list of all the new stuff, you can access the official Release Notes directly from inside Logic by selecting the Main Menu *Help ➤ Release Notes*, which opens your web browser, displaying the list on Apple's website.

https://support.apple.com/en-us/HT203718

 ### Why this Book?

So why did I write this book when all the new features and improvements are listed in the official Release Notes?

 #### Graphically Enhanced

The official Release Notes only provide a short one-line, text-only description of the new features and changes. In this book, I provide an in-depth explanation with lots of graphics, screenshots, diagrams, and sometimes additional detailed information of the topic to better understand the changes. You will immediately have a "clear picture" of the changes and additions and can start using them right away.

 #### Hidden Features

The official Release Notes often forget to list a few features, so whatever additional changes I stumbled over, found online, or what other users discovered on the various Logic forums, I will also include here.

### My other Logic Books

If you are new to my style of writing Graphically Enhanced Manuals and enjoy this book, don't forget to check out my other Logic books and my Graphically Enhanced Logic blog on my website http://LogicProGEM.com.

### Release Notes v10.3.2

This pdf file is **free**.

I make most of my Graphically Enhanced Release Notes books available for free to the Logic Pro community despite the fact that they are very time-consuming to produce. If you are familiar with my books, you know that I don't just deliver quick write-ups of existing release notes. I spend the time to research the various topics, use trial and error to understand how they work and create unique graphics and diagrams trying to find the best way to explain those new features and concepts beyond the information that is available from Apple.

Although this 10.3.2 version of Logic is just a minor release, it has quite a lot of features with new, sometimes not-so-easy concepts that required some extensive in-depth explanations to show how those new "toys" work. As you can see on the following pages, this turned out to be more work and time than expected with a total of over 80 pages.

I still decided to make this pdf available for free to get that information to as many Logic users as possible, so they can profit from all these great improvements and understand how to implement them in their Logic Projects. If you feel that the value you receive from my work is worth something to you, then it is up to you if you want to show some gratitude and contribute to my "*Starbuck Double Espresso Fund*" to help to keep me awake for future books to come.

Any contribution to my PayPal account **<sales@DingDingMusic.com>** is welcome. I appreciate it

*Disclaimer: Although I help Apple with my books to improve the knowledge and experience of their Logic Pro X customers, I don't get any compensation from Apple. Even if they want to, I'm not sure if Apple even has a PayPal account.*

## The GEM Advantage

If you've never read any of my other books and you aren't familiar with my Graphically Enhanced Manuals (GEM) series, let me explain my approach. As I mentioned at the beginning, my motto is:

### "UNDERSTAND, not just LEARN"

Other manuals (original User Guides or third party books) often provide just a quick way to: "press here and then click there, then that will happen ... now click over there, and something else will happen". This will go on for the next couple hundred pages, and all you'll do is memorize lots of steps without understanding the reason for doing them in the first place. Even more problematic is that you are stuck when you try to perform a procedure and the promised outcome doesn't happen. You will have no understanding why it didn't happen and, most importantly, what to do to make it happen.

Don't get me wrong, I'll also explain all the necessary procedures, but beyond that, the understanding of the underlying concept so you'll know the reason why you have to click here or there. Teaching you "why" develops a much deeper understanding of the application that later enables you, based on your knowledge, to react to "unexpected" situations. In the end, you will master the application.

And how do I provide that understanding? The key element is the visual approach, presenting easy to understand diagrams that describe an underlying concept better than five pages of text-only descriptions.

I mark important terms in this manual with a gray font. Try to memorize those terms or descriptions because that is the language you are using to communicate with other fellow Logic users or when asking questions or engaging in discussions on various Logic forums.

**The Visual Approach**

Here is a summary of the advantages of my Graphically Enhanced Manuals that set them apart from other books:

 **Better Learning**

 **Better Value**

☑ **Graphics, Graphics, Graphics**

Every feature and concept are explained with rich graphics and illustrations that are not found in any other book or User Guide, let alone YouTube videos. These are not just a few screenshots with arrows in it. I take the time to create unique diagrams to illustrate the concepts and workflows.

☑ **Knowledge and Understanding**

The purpose of my manuals is to provide the reader with the knowledge and understanding of an app that is much more valuable than just listing and explaining a set of features.

☑ **Comprehensive**

For any given feature, I list every available command so you can decide which one to use in your workflow. Some of the information is not even found in the app's User Guide.

☑ **For Beginners and Advanced Users**

The graphical approach makes my manuals easy to understand for beginners, but still, the wealth of information and details provide plenty of material, even for the most advanced user.

☑ **Three formats**

No other manual is available in all three formats: PDF (from my website), interactive multi-touch iBooks (on Apple's iBooks Store), and printed book (on Amazon).

☑ **Interactive iBooks**

No other manual is available in the enhanced iBooks format. I include an extensive glossary, also with additional graphics. Every term throughout the content of the iBook is linked to the glossary term that lets you pop up a little window with the explanations without leaving the page you are currently reading. Every term lists all the entries in the book where it is used and links to other related terms.

☑ **Up-to-date**

No other manual stays up to date with the current version of the app. Due to the rapid update cycles of applications nowadays, most books by major publishers are already outdated by the time they are released. I constantly update my books to stay current with the latest version of an app.

☑ **Free Updates** (pdf, iBook only)

No other manual provides free updates, I do. Whenever I update a book, I email a free download link of the pdf file to current customers. iBooks customers will receive an automatic update notification, and 24 hours after a new update, the printed book will be available on Amazon. They are print-on-demand books, which means, whenever you order a book on Amazon, you get the most recent version and not an outdated one that was sitting in a publisher's warehouse.

## Self-published

As a self-published author, I can release my books without any restrictions imposed by a publisher. Rich, full-color graphics and interactive books are usually too expensive to produce for such a limited audience. However, I have read mountains of manuals throughout the 35 years of my professional career as a musician, composer, sound engineer, and teacher, and I am developing these Graphically Enhanced Manuals (GEM) based on that experience, the way I think a manual should be written. This is, as you can imagine, very time consuming and requires a lot of dedication.

However, not having a big publisher also means not having a big advertising budget and the connections to get my books into the available channels of libraries, book stores, and schools. Instead, as a self-published author, I rely on reviews, blogs, referrals, and word of mouth to continue this series.

If you like my "Graphically Enhanced Manuals", you can help me promote these books by referring them to others and maybe taking a minute to write a review on Amazon or the iBooks Store.

Thanks, I appreciate it:

http://amzn.to/1sP8jvl        http://bit.ly/1oJ7ftQ

**Disclaimer**: As a non-native English speaker, I try my best to write my manuals with proper grammar and spelling. However, not having a major publisher also means that I don't have a big staff of editors and proofreaders at my disposal. So, if something slips through and it really bothers you, email me at <GrammarPolice@DingDingMusic.com>, and I will fix it in the next update. Thanks!

## LogicProGEM

Please check out my Logic site "**LogicProGEM.com**". The link "Blog" contains all the free Logic Articles that I have published on the web and continue to publish. These are in-depth tutorials that use the same concept of rich graphics to cover specific topics related to the use of Logic Pro X.

http://LogicProGEM.com

## Highlights

Here is the list of highlights of the new Logic Pro X v10.3.2 features, displayed on the following window when you first open the app.

This page is only displayed the first time when you launch the new update of the Logic app, but there is a command in the Main Menu *Help ▶ What's New in Logic Pro* that lets you open that window again .

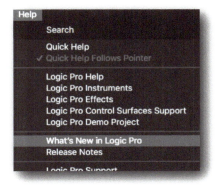

## Housekeeping

## New/Updated Sounds

After you've installed the Logic update and before diving into all the glory of the new changes and features, make sure to download any new or updated sounds that come with the update.

The following Menu Command *Logic Pro X ➤ Sound Library ➤ Download Updated Sounds* ❶ is only displayed if there are any updated sounds available that you haven't downloaded yet. The command opens the Sound Library Manager Window, and in the Status column, you will see the label "*Outdated*" ❷ or "*Incomplete*" ❸ for any sounds for the category that you need to update. Select those sound categories and *click* the "Install" button.

Make sure to check the indication ❹ at the bottom that tells you how much space you need on your drive for the download and installation.

*Attention*: The update is a two step process. First, Logic downloads an installer file that is hidden on your drive and then (after authorization), it installs the sounds from that installer file, which will be deleted after the successful installation. That means you need about twice the storage space of the actual download during the installation procedure.

## ➡ *Progress Bar*

During the download/installation pay attention to the LCD in the Logic Control Bar.

**Control Bar (LCD)**

▶ A blue line ❺ functions as a progress bar that moves from left to right, indicating the ongoing process.

▶ *Click* on the progress bar, and a popover ❻ appears with the information: what is downloaded, how much, and how long it takes until completion.

▶ The two buttons on the popover to the right ❼ let you either cancel ❎ or pause ⏸ the process.

▶ If you pause a process, an orange bar ❽ appears below the LCD to indicate that.

▶ The Pause button ⏸ has changed to an orange Resume button ❾ 🔄 that, you guessed it, lets you resume the process when you *click* on it.

BTW, this progress bar functionality already existed in 10.2.4

# Bug Fixes

Every Logic user has their own "favorite" bug (depending on their workflow), waiting to be fixed. Here are a few ones on the list:

- ☑ Automation of grouped tracks now works when Project Settings > MIDI > General > Control Change 7/10 controls Volume/Pan of channel strip objects setting is active.
- ☑ Volume automation resets as expected when a cycle returns to the beginning
- ☑ Undo now works after performing the Color Tracks by Region command.
- ☑ When a file that is being previewed in the Media tab is dragged into the Tracks area, it now stops playing back.
- ☑ It is again possible to set the Freeze mode for a track to Source Only in the Track Inspector.
- ☑ Printing from the Note Pad now defaults to black text on a white background.
- ☑ It is again possible to toggle the Metronome during recording when the "Only during count-in" option is enabled.
- ☑ External MIDI tracks now accurately follows the "Delay in milliseconds (ms)" track inspector setting when it is set to values below -100ms.
- ☑ Moving or copying flexed regions on grouped tracks will no longer shorten regions following the edits in some specific scenarios.
- ☑ Command-dragging a marker to the time ruler when the Global Tracks are closed now enables Cycle, as well as setting the locators to the range encompassed by the marker.
- ☑ Patches saved with plug-ins that use Software Instrument tracks as side chain inputs now properly recall the side chain setting when reloaded.
- ☑ Dual mono plug-ins saved as part of an Aux channel strip setting are no longer converted to stereo when the setting is reloaded.
- ☑ Low Latency mode now works as expected on Output channels above Output 1–2 that do not have plug-ins inserted on them.
- ☑ EXS24 now finds sampler Instruments as expected when there is an alias Sampler Instruments folder at the default location linked to a folder on an external drive.
- ☑ Selection-Based Processing applied to a marquee selected portion of a looped region now only affects the selected area.
- ☑ Software instrument tracks in duplicated Track Stacks now maintain their correct track names.

The Logic Pro X v10.3.2 update comes with lots of bug fixes (read through the full Release Notes), but if your "favorite" bug is still not fixed, keep on reporting it to the official feedback page at
http://www.apple.com/feedback/logic-pro.html

# Improvements

Besides the bug fixes, Logic updates usually include improvements regarding speed and responsiveness. This release is special in that regard because one major focus was responsiveness as we will see in the next chapter.

## GUI Redraw Speed Improvements

Let's start with the first improvement, which is not a flashy new feature, but, one of the most welcome improvement ...

**Speed of the Graphical User Interface (GUI).**

Many users were quite annoyed that Logic got kind of sluggish lately when it comes to screen redraws and overall responsiveness of the user interface (UI) and, therefore, one of the major requests was to make it snappy again. It seems that the developers listened and spent some time to improve the speed of many different types of screen redraws.

Of course, the speed improvements depend on the many factors of your Project and your specific hardware, but the underlying code is optimized to speed up any of the following actions. These speed improvements should be especially visible with larger screens and Retina displays.:

- ☑ Resizing views, window, Tracks, Global Tracks. The Playhead will disappear during resizing.
- ☑ Showing/Hiding Global Tracks
- ☑ Scrolling, especially "Momentum Scrolling" with Magic Mouse and Magic Trackpad.
- ☑ Trimming Regions
- ☑ Dragging Regions and Note Bars
- ☑ Dragging and moving the Cycle Range
- ☑ Drawing waveforms into Audio Regions
- ☑ Drawing Note Bars into MIDI Regions, especially the more notes there are and the smaller the available space
- ☑ Drawing the previous and next Region with crossfades, especially with a high track count and many Flex Markers
- ☑ Drawing Fades, especially at small horizontal and vertical zoom factors. The actual Fade Curve will be replaced by a simple ramp or vertical line
- ☑ Drawing Grid Lines in the background or the Workspace and the lines in the Ruler

Set the two sliders in the *System Preferences ➤ Keyboard* all the way to the right for the fastest response when using Key Commands for zooming (*cmd+ArrowLeft/Right/Up/Down*).

# Modified Drummer Interface

Before introducing the big new feature in 10.3.2, the three new Percussion Drummers, we have to first talk about the Drummer interface. Something has changed or at least moved around.

 ## Recap

The "Drummer" feature in Logic is not just a drum plugin that you load on your Track. Instead, it is more of an eco-system with many components working together.

The Logic developers tried to manage the balance between "ease of use" and "extremely powerful". On the surface, the Drummer is easy to use by just adding a Drummer Track to your Project and then adjusting a few play parameters. However, once you try to do a little bit more and peek under the hood, it gets very complex very fast. This is the part where the "extremely powerful" comes in. There are many different components involved in the Drummer eco-system with different concepts of the actual drum sound source and complex and highly flexible routing and mixing setups. You really have to know how all that plays together to stay on top of it and not get any surprises due to the lack of proper understanding of the underlying architecture.

I get into all those details in my book "Logic Pro X - How it Works" and provide in-depth explanations of the concepts, components, and rules. Here is a quick recap.

### The Drummer Eco-system

This is an overview of the Drummer eco-system:

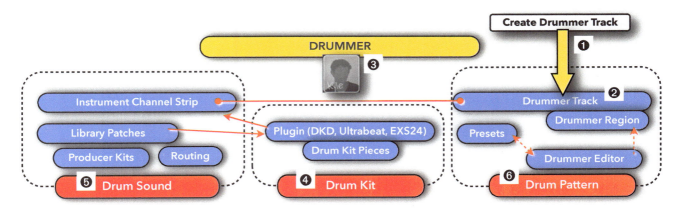

- **Create Drummer Track ❶**: The entire Drummer eco-system only exists on a Drummer Track ❷, which means it all starts with the command to create that special Drummer Track.

- **Drummer**: The key element of a Drummer Track is the actual "Drummer" ❸ also known as the Drummer Character. The important part to understand is that the 31 available Drummers (grouped in 7 Genres) are just macros. They load two elements, a specific Drummer Patch and a set of specific Drummer Presets. These two elements determine the three components that you can edit.

  - ☑ **Drum Kit** (Plugin) ❹: This is the component that determines the actual Drum Kit and the Drum Kit Pieces by tweaking the Software Instrument Plugin, the sound source of those drums.

  - ☑ **Drum Sound** (Mixer) ❺: This is the component where you control the sound of the Drum Kit on your Mixer via Channel Strips by configuring and routing those Channel Strips.

  - ☑ **Drum Pattern** (Editor) ❻: This is the component that determines what you play on the Drum Kit by configuring and editing the individual Drummer Region in the Drummer Editor.

## 🧑 Architecture Diagram

Here is another diagram that shows how the individual elements work together:

▶ **Drummer** (Macro) ❶: This is the important aspect to understand about the Drummer Character that you have to keep in mind whenever a Drummer is selected during the creation of a new Drummer Track ❷ or when you later select a Drummer Character ❸ from the Library Browser. It loads (overwrites) two elements, a Drummer Patch ❹ and a set of Drummer Presets ❺.

▶ **Drummer Patch** ❹: A Drummer Patch loads a specific Software Instrument ❻, i.e. a Drum Kit Designer, Ultrabeat (for Drum Machine Designer), or EXS24 (for the new Percussion Drummer). It also loads Channel Strip Settings ❼ (FX Plugins, Sends) and additional Channel Strips with specific routings.

  • Ignore Drummer Patch ❽: With the new padlock in the Library Browser, you can lock your current Drummer Patch, so a new Drummer will not overwrite those components.

▶ **Drummer Presets** ❺: The second element loaded by a Drummer is a set of Drummer Presets that are stored on your drive in the system library for each Drummer. These Presets are available from the Beat Presets List in the Drummer Editor when you select a Drummer Region on that Drummer Track. One important thing that also happens is that one of those Presets (the Default Drummer Preset) is loaded to each Drummer Region on that Drummer Track to become the Active Drummer Region, the one with the displayed Parameters in the Drummer Editor.

  • Ignore Active Drummer Preset ❾: If you have edited the Drummer Regions on a Drummer Track and you replace the Drummer ❶, you would overwrite those edits by loading the default Preset ❺ of that new Drummer. A setting in the Drummer Editor lets you prevent that ❾. You still load all the Presets for the new Drummer, but the current Drummer Region parameters are not changed.

▶ **Software Instrument Plugin** ❿: Keep in mind that you can edit the Drum Kit (Software Instrument Plugin) by loading a different Plugin Setting or Drum Kit Pieces from the Library or the Plugin Window ⓫ directly into the Software Instrument Plugin without changing anything else (i.e. Drummer Pattern, Drum Sound).

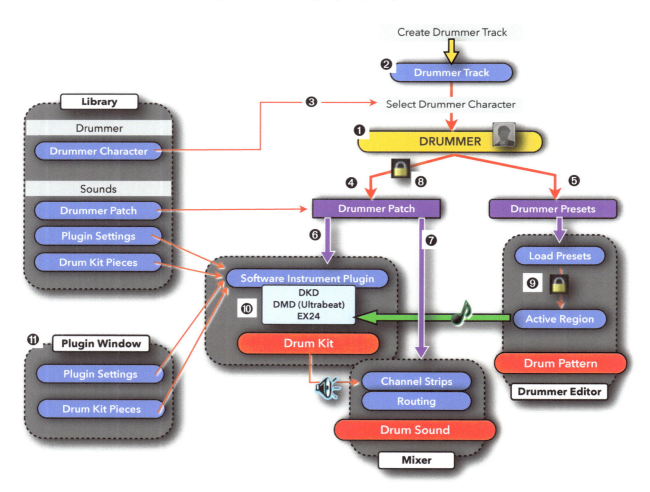

➡️ *New GUI*

With that diagram in mind, let's look at the modified Drummer Interface:

🌑 *10.3.1:*

The Drummer Editor ❶ shows three components of the currently selected Drummer Region ❷.

▶ **Drummer Character ❸**: The left side shows the selected Drummer that was loaded on the Drummer Track of the currently selected Drummer Region ❷. It provides all the controls to load a different Drummer (to the current Track).

▶ **Drummer Presets ❹**: To the left of the XY Pad is the Beat Presets List with the set of presets (Drummer Presets) that was loaded with that specific Drummer.

▶ **Play Parameter ❺**: The main area of the Drummer Editor provides the various play parameters.

🌑 *10.3.2:*

The left section with the Drummer Character has been relocated from the Drummer Editor to the Library ❻. Everything else in the Drummer Editor stays the same ❼.

**➡ Advanced**

In addition to just having the Drummer Section moved from the Drummer Editor to the Library, there are a few more details I want to demonstrate in this more advanced part. I'm sure many Logic users don't have a clear understanding of the full functionality (and the powerful features) of the Library Browser, i.e. what it actually displays (and when, depending on the tiny blue arrow on the Inspector Channel Strip), and also its hidden features like setting Default Patches or the extremely flexible Patch Merging (everything explained in "Logic Pro X - How it Works").

### 💡 Library - Loading Drummer

First, pay attention to the (up to) three sections in the Browser:

**Library Browser**

- ▶ **Icon Area ❶**: The Icon Area on top (with the label "*Library*") is always visible. You can vertically resize that area by **dragging** its divider line 🔀. With a Drummer Genre selected, it displays the following items:
    - • Drummer Character Card ❷. **Click** on it to toggle the Drummer Editor.
    - • Description of the Drummer ❸.
    - • When you move the mouse cursor over the Icon Area, a left ◀ and right ▶ arrow ❹ appears that let you load the next or previous Drummer of the current Genre.
- ▶ **Drummer Area ❺**: The Drummer Area with the label "*Drummer*" is only displayed in the Library when a Drummer Track is selected in the Tracks Area (aka the Arrange Window) The area has two columns.
    - • **Genre Column ❻**: The Genre on the left acts as a categories folder, listing all the 7 Genres, including the new Genre "*Percussion*". **Clicking** on a Genre will not load a Drummer, it only moves the key focus to the Drummer Area (category highlighted in blue ❼), lists all the Drummers for that genre, and display the currently loaded Drummer, same as in the Icon Area ❷ above.
    - • **Drummer Character Column ❽**: The right column displays all the available Drummers for the selected Genre. It lists the small Character Card with the Drummer Name followed by the music style. Be careful, **clicking** on an item in that column will load that Drummer, overwriting a lot of settings. An Alert Dialog warns you about that because there is no undo for that action.
- ▶ **Sounds Area ❾**: This is the default area that is always displayed in the Library Browser. It displays Patches, Channel Strip Settings, Plugin Settings, etc. Again, you have to dive into the functionality of the Library to fully understand how it works, so you are aware what is displayed in that Sounds Area. The screenshot of this example displays the following elements:
    - • The Sounds Area also has items selected (highlighted with gray ❿). This is important because it shows you what Drummer Patch has been loaded on the selected Track. Please note that this could be the default Drummer Patch for the specific Drummer selected in the Drummer Area above, but also could be a different Drummer Kit that you chose after selecting the Drummer. Again, this is the part where you have to keep in mind the somewhat complex architecture that I illustrated in the previous diagram.

## 🥁 Library - Loading Drummer Patch

As we have just seen on the previous page, when you load a Drummer in the Drummer Area of the Library, the Sounds Area below has its Drummer Patch (and its Patch Category) selected (highlighted in gray). This screenshot shows the same example, but now I have *clicked* on the "Drum Kit" category ❶ in the Sounds Area. Here is what will change:

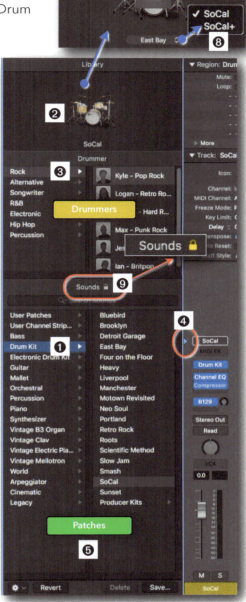

▶ **Change Drummer Patch**: At any time, you can load a different Drummer Patch on a Drummer Track, overwriting the default Drummer Patch of the originally loaded Drummer.

- ☑️ First, *click* on a Patch Category ❶ in the left column of the Sounds Area ("*Drum Kit*", "*Electronic* Drum *Kit*", or "*Percussion*").

- ☑️ The Sounds Area now has key focus, indicated by the blue highlighted "Drum Kit" category ❶.

- ☑️ Because the Sounds Area has key focus, the Icon Area on top now shows a Drum Kit Icon ❷ with the name of the Drummer Patch (i.e. "*SoCal*"). If you *clicked* on the Drummer Genre ❸ in the Drummer Area (change key focus), the Icon Area would change to the Drummer Character Card again like on the previous screenshot.

- ☑️ If you refer to the architecture diagram I showed earlier, choosing a new Drummer Patch will not change the Drummer itself. The Presets and the Drummer Regions are not affected. Only the Patch will be overwritten, which means the actual Drum Set and its routing. Keep in mind that when you load a Producer Kit or change from a DKD-based Patch to a DMD-base Patch, the Mixer setup and routing can change dramatically.

- ☑️ The Inspector Channel Strip shows that little blue triangle ❹ pointing at the Setting Menu Button, indicating that the currently selected items ❺ in the Sounds Area are Patches or Channel Strip Settings. I explain that functionality in a free tutorial on my website "*Library: Controlled by a Tiny, Mysterious Triangle*". http://bit.ly/1Hz0DWw

- ☑️ If you move the mouse cursor over the Icon Area ❷ in the Library, three elements will appear:

  - The two arrow buttons ◁ ▷ ❻ to step through the Patches.

  - The Plugin Window Button ❼ to open the Plugin Window for the current Software Instrument Plugin.

  - A selector shows the current Drummer Patch. *Click* on it to shows a menu ❽ with the default Patch for that Drummer plus its Producer Kit (alternate Drummer for DMD-based Drummer) to switch back to the Drummer's default setting or switch between Basic Kit and Producer Kit.

- ☑️ Next to the "Sounds" label is a new padlock ❾ that is only displayed in the Library when a Drummer Track is selected. This is a button that, when *clicked* on, toggles between on 🔒 and off 🔓. It has the same function as the menu item under the Gear Button ⚙️▾ in the Drummer Editor ❿ "*Keep drum kit when changing drummers*". It protects the current Drummer Patch from being overwritten when you select a Drummer which would load its own default Drummer Patch.

### 🥁 Library/Plugin Window - Loading Drummer Plugin Settings

There is another level where you affect a Drummer, and it gets really confusing when you don't pay attention to which component it is affecting.

▶ **Drummer Area**: This screenshot shows the same example. A Drummer Track is selected, and that's why you see the Drummer Area ❶ in the Library Browser.

▶ **Blue Triangle**: You move the tiny blue triangle ❷ to the Instrument Slot Button ❸, in this example, loaded with the Drum Kit Designer. You do that by either *clicking* left of the button or *sh+clicking* on it.

▶ **Sounds Area**: Now the Sounds Area of the Library Browser displays Plugin Settings ❹ instead of Patches, which is a little detail that is very important (please note that if an EXS24 Instrument is loaded on the Instrument Slot, the Sounds Area will show the available "EXS Sampler Instruments"!).

▶ If you look at the names of the Plugin Settings ❹, you would recognize the same names for the Drummer Patches we just saw. This is one of the reasons why it is so easy to confuse those two settings for Drummers (Patches vs. Plugin Settings) and why you have to pay special attention.

  • **Patch**: A Patch includes the settings for the entire Channel Strip plus optional routing information. That means it could load additional Channel Strips (Aux Returns).

  • **Plugin Setting**: A Plugin Setting only includes the setting of a specific Plugin. In our case, selecting a Plugin Setting would only change the part of the Drummer Patch that loads the Plugin for the Drum Kit, but no other settings on that current Channel Strip or any other Channel Strip related to the loaded Drummer Patch would be affected.

▶ **Plugin Window**: You can open the Plugin Window of the currently loaded Plugin (in our example the Drum Kit Designer) by *clicking* on the Instrument Slot Button ❸ or by moving the mouse cursor over the icon in the Icon Area, which will show the Plugin Window Button ❺ that you can *click* on.

▶ **Drum Kit Pieces**: On the Plugin Window (for a DrumKitDesigner-based Drummer) you can adjust and change the individual Drum Kit Pieces by *clicking* on the picture to have the sidebars appear. For DrumMachineDesigner-based and EXS-based Drummers, the functionality is different.

▶ **Plugin Settings Menu**: If you *click* on the selector ❻ in the upper-left corner next to the big Power Button, another piece of the confusing puzzle appears, the Plugin Settings Menu. This menu (under the Factory submenu if you have already created custom Plugin Settings), again lists a whole set of Drum Kit Names. These are identical to the Plugin Settings displayed in the Library ❹ and you can choose those setting in either place, just know where and what they.

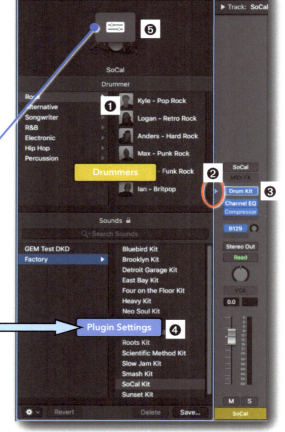

**Plugin Window**

# New Drummer Genre - Percussion

Logic 10.3.2 adds three new Drummers for a total of now 31 Drummers.

As we have seen in the previous section, the whole topic of Drummers can get very complex if you dig a little bit deeper and start to modify specific elements. Therefore, I also divided this section into two part, first the simplified introduction of the feature, what it is and how to use it and in the advanced part, I will dig a little bit deeper.

 **_Simplified_**

What you need to know about the new Drummers:

 **_New Drummer Genre "Percussion"_**

When opening the Track Select Dialog (***opt+cmd+N***) and select the Track Type _Drummer_ ❶, you will notice a new item in the Genre popup menu, "**Percussion**" ❷. Select that Genre and Logic creates a new Drummer Track with one of the three new Percussion Drummers selected, "_Isabela_" ❸.

**Track Select Dialog**

 **_3 New Drummers_**

Once the Drummer Track is created, you can see in the Drummer Area ❸ of the Library Browser (now with the new interface), the new _Percussion_ category ❹ on the left and the three new Drummers ❺ in that category on the right with Isabela _selected_ (the default Drummer in the Percussion genre).

These are the three new Percussion Drummers:

**Isabela** (Latin Percussion)

_Inspired by multicultural sounds from her hometown of Miami, Isabela plays fiery, dynamic rhythms on Latin percussion._

**Quincy** (Pop Percussion)

_A veteran of the studio and stage, Quincy plays straight forward, versatile percussion grooves that compliment pop, rock, and R&B._

**Finn** ( Songwriter Percussion)

_Finn replaced his drum kit with cajon, foot stomps, and hand claps to create stripped-down, organic beats perfect for acoustic songwriters._

**Library Browser**

## 🥁 *Drummer Editor*

You toggle the Drummer Editor ❶ (the window pane at the bottom of Logic's Main Window) by *double-clicking* on a Drummer Region ❷ or by *clicking* on the Editors Button ✂ ❸ on the Control Bar when a Drummer Region is selected.

### ▶ A word about the Drummer Editor

Please note that, unlike the MIDI Editors, the Drummer Editor only provides various play parameters ❹ that you can adjust. The combination of those play parameters determines a specific drum pattern for the currently select Drummer Region ❷ and when you play back that Drummer Region that drum pattern generates the actual MIDI Events that are sent in real time to the Software Instrument Plugin ❺ on that Track (Drum Kit Designer, Ultrabeat, or EXS24) which plays the drum pattern so you can hear it. Changing the play parameters ❷ for a selected Drummer Region changes its drum pattern.

### ▶ Different Play Parameters (Drummer Editor Interface)

Another little detail to be aware of is that the Drummer Editor has two different views for the play parameters. One is used for Drummer Patches that are based on the Drum Kit Designer (DKD) Plugin ❻ and the other one for Drummer Patched that are based on the Drum Machine Designer (DMD) ❼. The three new Percussion Drummers use the same Drummer Editor interface as the DMD-based Drummers.

## 💀 *Play Parameters*

Here is a quick overview of the play parameters of the three new Percussion Drummers:

▶ **Beat Presets ❶**: Each Drummer has a set of its own Drummer Presets (pre-configured patterns) that are loaded when you choose a specific Drummer. The Beat Presets List shows the available Presets, and the Gear Button ❷ ⚙▾ opens a popup menu for managing those Presets.

▶ **XY Pad ❸**: Position the yellow puck to determine the Complexity and Loudness of the pattern.

▶ **Instrument Groups ❹**: All the available percussion instruments are organized into three groups. You can *click* on an instrument icon to toggle them on (highlighted icon) or off (dimmed icon). The Variation Slider lets you set each of the three groups individually to any of the six playing variations. As you can see on the instrument icons, the three Percussion Drummers have different sets of percussion instruments ❺ ❻ ❼.

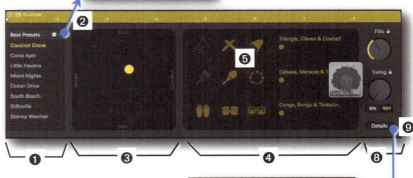

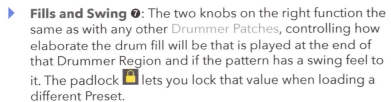

▶ **Fills and Swing ❼**: The two knobs on the right function the same as with any other Drummer Patches, controlling how elaborate the drum fill will be that is played at the end of that Drummer Region and if the pattern has a swing feel to it. The padlock 🔒 lets you lock that value when loading a different Preset.

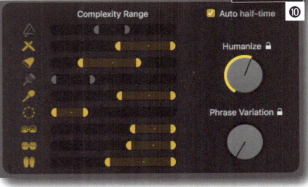

▶ **Details ❿**: *Click* on the "Details" Button ❾ to toggle the Instrument Groups Area ❹ to display the following parameters:

- **Complexity Range Sliders**: You can offset the Complexity value that you set with the XY Pad ❸. *Dragging* the left and right handles of the slider lets you set the range of the value changes and *dragging* the center of the slider lets you position it on the Complexity scale from left to right. *Click* on the instrument icon on the left to bypass that control.

- **Auto half-time Checkbox**: Enable the Audio half-time checkbox to play the pattern in half-time (half the Project Tempo).

- **Humanize Knob**: The Humanize Knob lets you add an amount of small timing offsets to the pattern to create a more realistic performance instead of having each note perfectly quantized.

- **Phrase Variation Knob**: The Phrase Variation Knob controls the number of rhythmic changes of the drum pattern throughout the length of the Drummer Region.

## ➡️ *Advanced*

Now let's look at some more advanced features of the new Percussion Drummers.

### 🙂 *New Patch Category "Percussion"*

Here is a screenshot of the Library Browser and based on what we reviewed earlier, we can now better understand what we see:

- ▶ The Sounds Area ❶ in the Library Browser has a new Patch Category named "*Percussion*" ❷.
- ▶ The Percussion Category includes three Patches ❸, which are the Drummer Patches that are loaded when you select one of the three Percussion Drummers ❹ listed above in the Drummer Area ❺:
  - **Isabela** ➤ Latin
  - **Quincy** ➤ Studio
  - **Finn** ➤ Coffee Shop
- ▶ The Percussion Category also includes two folders ❻ "*Producer Kits*" and "*Performance Patches*" that I explain later.

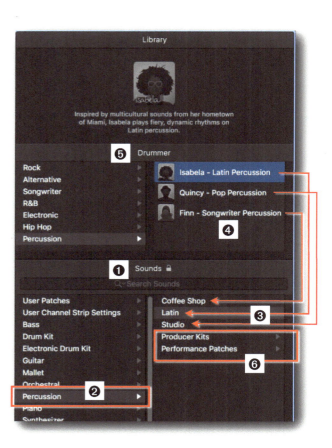

Remember, a "Drummer" ❼ is just a macro, a set of instructions, that loads a Drummer Patch ❽ and a set of Drummer Presets ❾ onto a Drummer Track. The difference between the 31 Drummers in Logic is that they load different Drummer Patches and different sets of Drummer Presets, that's it.

If you think about it, those three new Percussion Drummers ❹ just represent three new Drummer Patches ❸ (*Latin*, *Studio*, *Coffee Shop*) and three new sets of Drummer Presets for those Drummers. Keep in mind that you can use those Drummer Patches to load them onto any other Drummer Track ❿ or any Software Instrument Track if you want to play and record them with your external MIDI controller.

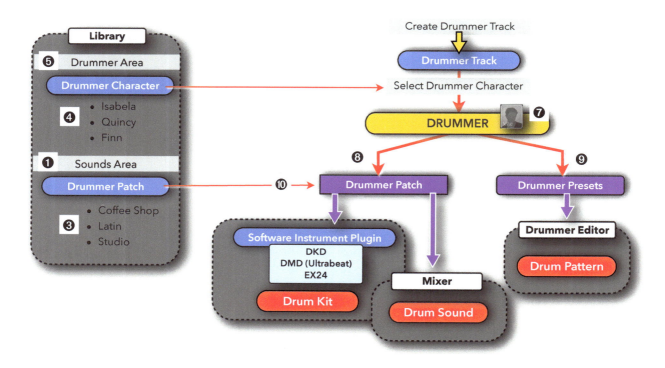

### *Drummer Patches*

Saying that the new Percussion Drummers just represent new Drummer Patches would be an understatement because those Drummer Patches have some new and different stuff inside that's worth looking at. Be warned, if you thought that the underlying routing concept of Drummers was complex before, then embrace yourself, because it will get even more complicated.

Similar to the Drummers that are based on the Drum Kit Designer ("DKD-based"), the Drummer Patches for the Percussion Drummers also come in two variations, Basic Kits and Producer Kits.

#### 🥁 Basic Kits

Selecting any of the three Percussion Drummers will load a Basic Kit. These are the three Drummer Patches ❶ you see in the Library.

**Library Browser**

Those three Drummer Patches that load a Basic Kit create the following elements (open the Mixer to see it):

- ☑ **Instrument Channel Strip ❷**: This is an Instrument Channel Strip assigned to the Drummer Track (or any Track you load that Drummer Patch to).

- ☑ **EXS24 Instrument Plugin ❸**: The Instrument Channel Strip has an EXS24 Instrument Plugin loaded with a Sampler Instrument ❹ that contains all the mapping to the percussion samples. More about that in a minute.

- ☑ **Audio FX**: The Channel Strip also has various Audio FX ❻ loaded for sound processing.

- ☑ **Aux Channel Strip**: In addition to the Instrument Channel Strip, the Patch also creates a new Aux Channel Strip ❼ that functions as an Aux Return with a Reverb Plugin ❽, bussed ❾ from the Instrument Channel Strip.

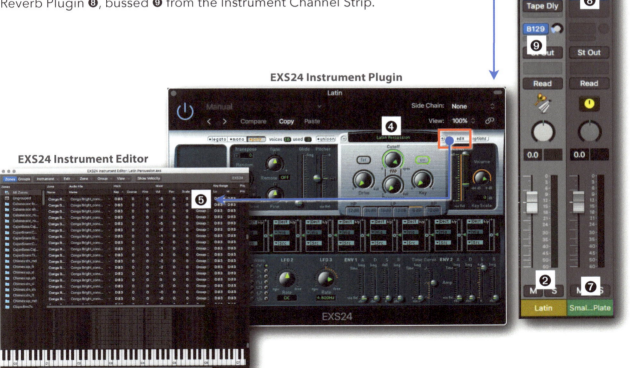

**EXS24 Instrument Plugin**

**EXS24 Instrument Editor**

And now, let's dig even a little bit deeper:

Remember, the Sounds Area in the Library Browser can display various settings (Patches, Channel Strip Settings, Plugin Settings, etc.). To know which one you are looking at in the Library Browser depends on the currently selected Track Type and the position the tiny blue triangle ▮▶ is pointing at in the Inspector Channel Strip.

Look at the screenshot of a Drummer Track to understand all the bits and pieces:

▸ The Percussion Drummer "*Isabela*" ❶ is loaded as you can see in the Drummer Area of the Library because that Drummer is selected.

▸ On the Inspector Channel Strip, I have *sh+clicked* the Instrument Slot Button ❷ to position the tiny blue arrow next to it.

▸ When the blue arrow points at the Instrument Plugin Slot (or any Audio FX Plugin Slots), then the Sounds Area in the Library ❸ will not display Patches, and instead, displays the Plugin Settings for that Plugin.

▸ *Attention*: There is one exception to that rule, and that is what we have here. If the Instrument Plugin is an EXS24, then the Sounds Area ❸ will display all the Sampler Instruments ❹ of the EXS24 and not its Plugin Settings (that you can still access from its Plugin Setting Menu).

▸ These Sampler Instruments ❹ (with their folder hierarchy) are the same that you can access from the EXS24 Menu ❺ when *clicking* on its Sampler Instruments Menu ❻.

▸ Remember, even after loading a specific Drummer ❼ that loads its corresponding Drummer Patch ❽ with its corresponding EXS Sampler Instrument ❾, you can manually load a different Drummer Patch (which loads its corresponding EXS Sampler Instrument ❽), and even then, you can load a different EXS Sampler Instrument ❾.

▸ The Sampler Instruments are stored in the Finder ❿ at the following location: */Library/ Application Support/Logic/Sampler Instruments/ 03 Drums & Percussion/05 Percussion*

Always make sure to know what you are looking at before selecting something!

| ❼ Drummer | ❽ Drummer Patch | ❾ EXS Sampler Instrument |
|---|---|---|
| **Isabela** | Latin | Latin Percussion |
| **Quincy** | Studio | Studio Percussion |
| **Finn** | Coffee Shop | Coffee Shop Percussion |

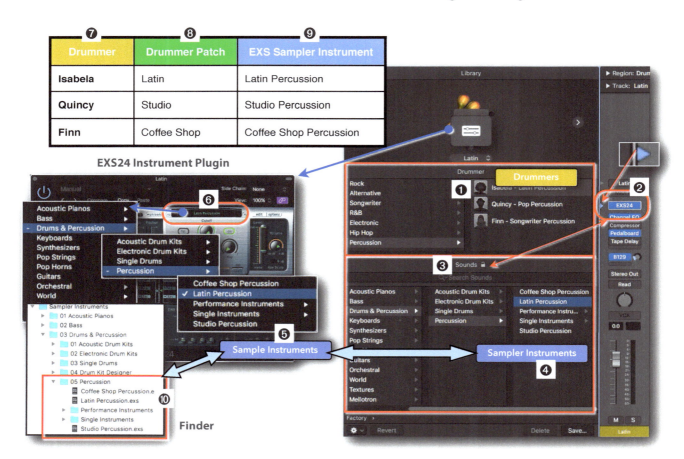

EXS24 Instrument Plugin

Finder

## 🥁 *Producer Kits*

Fasten your seat belts, because this is where the fun starts.

After switching the Sounds Area ❶ of the Library Browser back to display the Patches, we now *click* on the *Producer Kits* category ❷ (a folder), that shows seven Drummer Patches ❸, all ending with the plus sign (+). This is the same concepts as with the DKD-based Producer Kits.

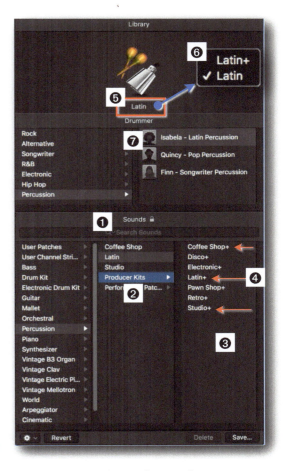

▶ Drummer Patches with the + sign indicate that this is a Producer Kit.

▶ Each of the three new Drummer Patches ❹ for the Percussion Drummers exists inside the Producer Kits folder with the same name and the plus sign at the end.

- Latin+
- Studio+
- Coffee Shop+

▶ There are four additional Drum Patches that only exist as Producer Kits.

- Disco+
- Electronic+
- Pawn Shop+
- Retro+

▶ You can switch between a Basic Kit and its corresponding Producer Kit by directly selecting the Patch in the Sounds Area, or *click* on the Patch Name Label ❺ in the Icon Area, which opens a menu ❻ listing the Basic Kit and Producer Kit of the currently loaded Drummer. Please note that this menu is only displayed when the Sounds Area ❶ has key focus and not the Drummer Area ❼!

### Wow!

If you wonder what the difference is between a Basic Kit ❽ and a Producer Kit ❾, here is a screenshot. The Producer Kit version of Drummer Patches in the Percussion category creates a mixer setup of up to 39 Channel Strips. Remember, this is single Patch!

Also remember, switching between a Basic Kit and a Producer Kit doesn't change anything regarding the Drummer Regions, the Drummer Editor, or the Drummer Presets. It only affects the routing of that instrument, determining whether the percussion set is represented by a single Channel Strip or if every Percussion Kit Piece in that set is routed to its individual Channel Strip with additional Aux Returns.

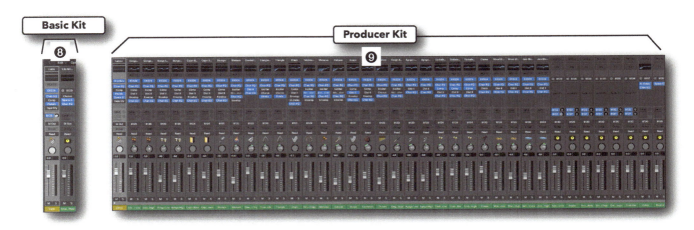

## Producer Kit = a Nested Summing Stack

The mixer layout for the Producer Kit of a Percussion Patch is similar to the Drum Machine Designer Patches.

▸ **Special Summing Stack**: The Drummer Patch is based on a special Summing Stack, which I call "*DMD Summing Stack*"

▸ **Main Track ❶**: The Main Track of this Summing Stack is an Aux Channel Strip with the Drum Machine Designer "Plugin" as its input. Remember, this is not actually a Plugin, it functions as a special Bus return (Main Bus) that also has its own user interface, the Drum Machine Designer Window.

▸ **EXS24 Channel Strips ❷**: There are 29 Instrument Channel Strips, each one with a separate EXS24 Instrument Plugin. Please note that the DKD-based Patches use a single Drum Kit Designer instance with its multi-outputs routed to separate Aux Channel Strips. The similar concept of the DMD-based Patches uses a single instance of a multi-output Ultrabeat. The setup for Percussion-based Patches, however, uses 29 <u>individual instances</u> of EXS24

Plugins loaded on 29 separate Instrument Channel Strips (despite the fact that the EXS24 also has multi-output capabilities).

▸ **Drum Group Channel Strips**: The output of the 29 individual EXS24 Channel Strips ❸ are routed to (spread over) 6 busses that are returned on 6 Aux Channel Strips ❺, functioning as audio subgroups, each one representing a specific instrument group (congas, bongos, tambourine, etc.).

▸ **FX Channel Strips**: Each of the 6 Drum Groups has two Aux Sends ❻ that function as FX busses sent to two Aux Channel Strips ❼ with Audio FX loaded (Reverb, Delay).

▸ **Main Bus**: Only the output of the six Drum Group Channel Strips ❽ and the output of the two FX Channel Strips ❾ are routed via a bus ❿ (Main Bus) to the input of the Main Track ❶ that functions as the Master Channel Strip for this huge Summing Stack.

**Percussion+: Summing Stack Routing**

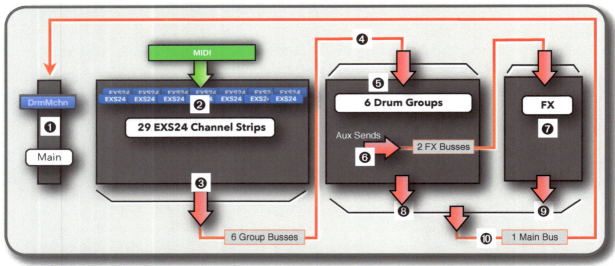

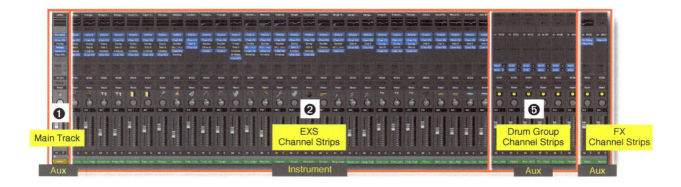

     3 - New Big Features

## Single Instruments

The purpose of having those big Producer Kits is to route each Drum Kit Piece of a Drum Kit or Percussion Kit to its own Channel Strip so you can set their levels separately and individually process them with Audio FX Plugin and Sends on those Channel Strips. As we have just seen, the new Percussion-based Drummer Patches use a different concept to route the individual Drum Kit Pieces to their separate Channel Strips:

- ▶ **Single Plugin with Multi-outputs**: DMD-based Patches and Producer Kits of DKD-based Patches use a single instance of a Sampler Instrument Plugin (Drum Kit Designer or Ultrabeat) in Multi-output Mode. The individual Drum Kit Pieces are sent to the additional audio outputs of the Plugin, which are routed to separate Aux Channel Strips so that you can process them independently.

- ▶ **Multiple Plugins**: The Producer Kits of Percussion-based Patches use multiple EXS24 Instrument Plugins. Each Instrument Channel Strip has a separate instance of an EXS Plugin loaded.

Here is the concept:

- The Producer Kit of a Percussion-based Patch has 29 (or more) Instrument Channel Strips ❶.

- Each Channel Strip has an EXS24 Plugin loaded in Stereo Mode (not Multi-output Mode!) ❷

- Logic 10.3.2 has 41 new .exs Sampler Instruments for the EXS24, each one having only a single Percussion Kit Piece mapped to a single key.

- Those Sampler Instruments are located in the Finder ❸ at */Library/Application Support/Logic/Sample Instruments/03 Drums & Percussion/05 Percussion/Single Instrument*

- In the EXS24 Plugin Window, you can navigate to that folder from the Sampler Instrument Menu ❹ to the *Single Instruments* folder ❺ listing all the EXS Sampler Instrument ❻

- The special DMD Summing Stack that the Producer Kit is using enables the Main Track ❼ to route the individual MIDI Notes (c1, c#1, d1, etc.) that the Drummer Track generates (or you play on the external MIDI controller) to the individual Channel Strips that has that Sampler Instrument loaded with that specific Percussion Kit Piece (conga low, conga, high, etc.) assignment.

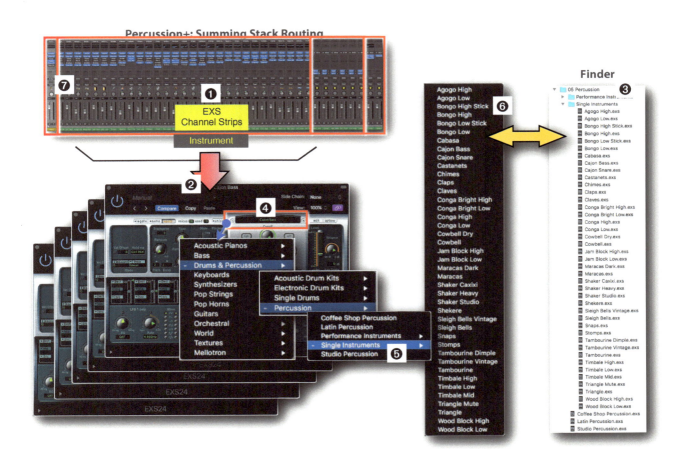

Percussion+: Summing Stack Routing

## Drum Machine Designer (DMD) Window

The Producer Kit of the Percussion-based Drummer Patches uses the same Drum Machine Designer Window that is also used in DMD-based Drummer Patches with similar functionality.

- ▶ **Functionality**: You use this window as quick access to the important controls of the 39 Channel Strips of the Summing Stack without the need of opening the stack in the mixer.
- ▶ **Show/Hide**: Toggle the window by *double-clicking* on the Track Icon ❶ of the Main Track in the Track Header or *clicking* the Input Button (labeled "*DrmMchn*" ❷) of the corresponding Channel Strip.
- ▶ The lower pane of the DMD Window has different views with different controls:
  - **Main Controls**: If the Window Header ❸ is selected (on top, displaying the Patch Name), then the lower half of the window shows either the six Volume Knobs and Mute Buttons for the six Drum Group Channels ❹ and six Smart Controls ❺ that affect the Audio FX Plugin on the Main Track ❻ (when the Controls Button is selected), or it shows the Aux Sends of the six Drum Groups ❼ for the Delay and Reverb (when the Sends Button is selected).
  - **Instrument Controls**: If you select any of the Cells ❽ in the upper half of the DMD Window (there are three views you can step through to access all 48 Cells), then the lower pane displays eight knobs ❾ that control various parameters of that specific EXS24 Plugin control of that Channel Strip. Remember, each Cell represents a different EXS24 Instrument Plugin in the Mixer that has that specific Kit Piece loaded (represented by the name and icon of the Cell).

## DMD Window and Smart Controls Window

If you ever wondered what those controls in the lower pane of the Drum Machine Designer Window really are, then let's open another advanced layer and look at the Smart Controls.

▶ In the Tracks Area of Logic's Main Window, select the Main Track ❶ of the Percussion-based Producer Kit and open the Smart Controls ❷ (*B*) ⚙.

▶ There are two buttons ❸ in the middle of the Menu Bar, "*Controls*" and "*Sends*". These are the same two buttons we just saw on the Drum Machine Designer Window.

▶ Selecting a button will show the same user interface ❹ as on the DMD Window.

▶ When you open the Smart Controls Inspector ❺ on the left (by *clicking* on the I-Button ⓘ in the upper-left corner of its Menu Bar, you can see the parameters and control ❻ to configure those Smart Controls. This is the place where you can edit/configure the controls, and because those controls in the Smart Controls window are the same as the DMD Window, you can customize the DMD Window this way.

▶ If you *click* on a Subtrack ❼ in the Tracks Area, which represents one of the Instrument Channel Strips that has an EXS24 loaded, then the Smart Controls Window changes to display the other 8 knobs ❽ we just saw on the DMD Window.

▶ Again, look at the Smart Controls Inspector ❾ and you'll find all the configurations for those knobs ❿. *Click* on the different knobs and follow their sophisticated configurations. These are not just one-on-one assignments, many are complex macros, controlling multiple parameters at the same time. I show all the details how to create Smart Controls in my book "Logic Pro X - How it Works".

## Swapping Percussion Kit Pieces

Swapping Percussion Kit Pieces is one more (very advanced) procedure you can do with a Producer Kit of the Percussion-based Drummer Patches. You will understand the following better if you already know how to swap Drum Kit Pieces for a DMD-based Drummer Patch.

▶ ***Click*** on a Cell ❶ in the DMD Window and see what happens in the Inspector Channel Strip and the Library Browser.

▶ The Left Inspector Channel Strip ❷ shows the Main Track of this Summing Stack and the Right Inspector Channel Strip ❸ shows the Subtrack. This is one of the special functions of the Right Inspector Channel Strip that I demonstrate in my free tutorial http://bit.ly/2sVdeFg.

▶ The important thing to understand is that each Cell ❶ on the DMD Window represents a single Instrument Channel Strip ❸ (of that Summing Stack) with an EXS24 Plugin ❹ that has one of the 41 EXS24 Sampler Instruments loaded (listed in the "Single Instruments" category that I showed pages earlier). The name on the Cell is the name of the Channel Strip ❸ and the name of that EXS Sample Instrument.

▶ Please note that the tiny blue triangle ❺ now is pointing at the Setting Button of the Right Inspector Channel Strip. That means that the Sounds Area ❻ of the Library Browser now displays the Patches for that Channel Strip ❼ and as you can see, a Patch with the same name "Cajon Bass" is currently selected.

▶ The Sounds Area shows where those Patches are stored *Electronic Drum Kit ➤ Drum Machine Designer ➤ Kit Pieces ➤ Acoustic Percussion ➤*. Please note that the bottom of the Sounds Area shows the path name ❽ if you don't have enough columns in the Sounds Area.

▶ ***Clicking*** on any of those Patches ❼ in the Library will load that Patch onto the selected Cell ❶ and, therefore, replaces that Channel Strip with all its configuration (i.e. Audio FX).

▶ The DMD Window has a total of 48 Cells (over three pages), and some of the Cells are empty. Just ***click*** on an empty Cell and select one of those 41 Patches ❼.

▶ Please note that what you see here ❼ are 41 Patches (.patch files stored inside the Logic application) with the same name as the 41 Sampler Instruments (.exs files stored in the system library), but they are two different things/files with a different purpose. That's why you have to have a solid understanding of those underlying concepts before using any of the advanced techniques, or it gets really confusing.

▶ One more thing. You can use the Mute and Solo Button ❾ on a Cell and also ***ctr+click*** on it to open its Shortcut Menu ❿. However only the "*Clear Cell*" command works. The "*Create Track*" command is redundant because the Percussion-based Producer Kits have Tracks already assigned to each Cell.

## Performance Patches

There is a special Patch Category listed in the Sounds Area of the Library Browser named "*Performance Patches*" ❶. Be careful, because those Patches are not to be used on Drummer Tracks.

To better understand that, let's review what the term "Drummer" means in Logic

> A **Drummer**
>
> is a macro (a set of instructions) that loads
>
> a **Drummer Patch** and a set of **Drummer Presets**
>
> onto a **Drummer Track**

▶ **Drummer Track ❷**: Logic has a lot of Drummer Patches in the Library Browser that are automatically loaded onto a Drummer Track when you select a specific Drummer. These Drummer Patches load Sampler Plugins (Drum Kit Designer, Ultrabeat, EXS24) that are configured so their samples (the Drum or Percussion Kit Pieces) are correctly mapped for the Drummer Track. Think about the standardized mapping that General MIDI is using.

▶ **Instrument Track ❸**: All the Drummer Patches are not reserved just for Drummer Tracks. You can load any of those Patches onto an Instrument Track and play them with your external MIDI controller and record those MIDI Events. Remember, you can play back MIDI Regions on a Drummer Track, but you cannot record MIDI on a Drummer Track.

The basic rule about Drummer Tracks is that you can only load Patches onto them that are specifically configured regarding their sample-mapping. Technically, you could load any Patch onto a Drummer Track, but that is more of an experimental hit-and-miss situation to see what samples are triggered by the drum pattern that is generated based on the parameter settings for a specific Drummer Region.

The 11 Patches ❹ in the *Performance Patches* Category ❶ of the Library are Patches that are meant to be loaded onto Instrument Tracks ❸ and not Drummer Tracks ❷. They create a Channel Strip with an EXS24 Plugin loaded with an .exs Sampler Instruments with the same name ❺, located in the library directory. These Patches are useful if you just want to play a specific percussion instrument (i.e. congas, timbales, etc.) with all its available variations and nuances.

# Loop Browser Changes

The Loop Browser, at least the upper part, has a few cosmetic and functional changes.

 **10.3.1**

The Loop Browser in 10.3.1 had three areas:

▸ **Search Pane ❶**: The upper part of the browser provides various controls to make a search selection. It provides two different views to make the selection, the Button View and the Column View.

▸ **Results Pane ❷**: The lower part of the browser displays the results, all the Apple Loops that meet the search criteria made in the Search Pane above.

▸ **Status Bar**: The bar at the bottom of the Loop Browser has some playback controls and a number that shows how many items are displayed in the Results Pane.

 **10.3.2**

What has changed in 10.3.2 is the Search Pane, especially the interface for the Button View, plus some controls have been re-arranged. Instead of four, now there are three sections in the Search Pane:

▸ **First ❸**: The section on top now contains the two toggle buttons to switch between Button View and Column View plus the Loop Packs Selector. Its label has been renamed from "Loops" to "Loop Packs".

▸ **Second ❹**: The second section now displays the Button View or the Column View. The default view is the Button View, which has changed quite a bit.

▸ **Third ❺**: This section now displays the Scale Selector, the Signature Selector, and the Search Field.

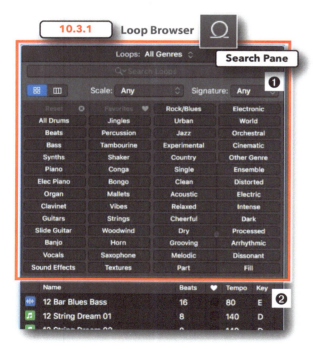

### 🐢 The New Button View

The interface and functionality of the Button View now work the following way with a lot of little details:

▶ **Button View Button**: The button for the Button View has changed from ⊞ to ▭.

▶ **Main Buttons**: In 10.3.1 all the buttons for various Instruments, Genre, and Modes, plus the Favorite and the Reset button, were always displayed. You only could resize that window pane itself. Now in 10.3.2, you have five main buttons:

- ❶ Reset ✕
- ❷ **Instrument** (Show/Hide Instrument Buttons)
- ❸ **Genre** (Show/Hide Genre Buttons)
- ❹ **Moods** (Show/Hide Moods Buttons)
- ❺ **Favorite** ♡

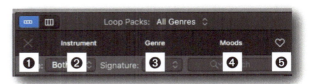

▶ **Show/Hide Categories**: *Click* on any of the three Show/Hide Category Buttons ❻ (*Instrument*, *Genre*, *Moods*) and it turns blue, extending the Button View to show the corresponding buttons underneath ❼. *Click* again to hide those buttons. *Clicking* on one Show/Hide Instrument Button will select that button and deselect any of the other two Show/Hide Instrument Buttons.

▶ *Cmd+click* on any of the three Show/Hide Category Buttons to select/deselect that button without affecting the show/hide status of any of the other two Show/Hide Buttons ❽. The Search Pane just extends further to show all those displayed Category Buttons ❾.

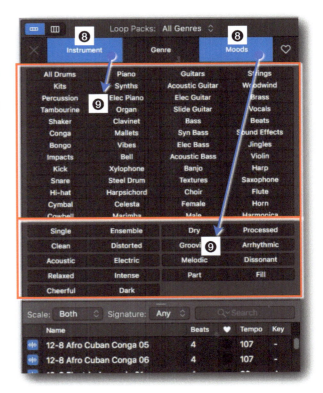

▶ **Category Selection**: When you select any of the Category Buttons, that selection is then displayed on the Show/Hide Category Buttons even if the categories are hidden ❶. It provides only one line, so if you have multiple selections that don't fit on one line, you will see the three dots ...

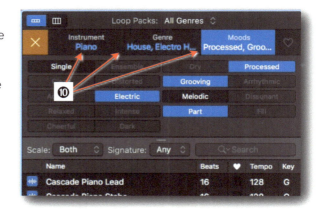

▶ ❷ **Favorite Button** ♡ : You can select the Favorite Button in addition to any selection to restrict the search to Apple Loops that have been flagged as Favorite ❸. The button is grayed out if the current selection doesn't include any Apple Loops with the Favorite flag.

▶ ❹ **Reset Button** ✕ : The Reset Button turns brown (active) any time you have made a selection. *Click* on the button and the current selection will be reset and the Reset Button turns gray again.

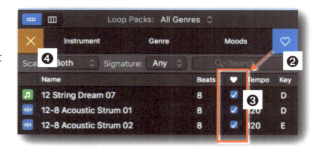

▶ **Reassign Buttons**: Reassigning buttons works similar as before. *Ctr+click* on an Instrument Button ❺, and a Shortcut Menu with submenus lets you select a new Instrument ❻ to assign it to that button. This procedure only works for Instruments but not for Genres anymore, because all the 23 Genre Buttons are always displayed when the Show/Hide Genre Button is selected.

# Yellow Apple Loops

## ➡ Recap

Very often you can hear professional composers talking down on Apple Loops as something only a beginner or a non-musician would use to put together some tracks. Unfortunately, this attitude is kind of silly because they are missing out on an amazing tool for composing, whether it is for quick sketching out some sections or as raw material to play around with in all kinds of bent shapes and forms.

So far, we had Blue Apple Loops and Green Apple Loops, available in the Loop Browser.  Here are few things you should know about them:

- ▸ Both types of Apple Loops are audio files, special audio files with additional data and metadata.

- ▸ **Blue Apple Loops** (or "Audio Loops") only contain an audio file (in addition to some metadata) and can only be placed on Audio Tracks.

- ▸ **Green Apple Loops** (or "MIDI Loops") contain an audio file and, also, the MIDI data and the Channel Strip Settings of the Software Instrument Track that created that loop. Therefore, Green Apple Loops can be placed on Audio Tracks (using its audio file), or on Software Instrument Tracks (placing the MIDI data into a MIDI Region and loading the Software Instrument Plugin that plays that Region).

## ➡ New Yellow Apple Loops

- ▸ **Yellow Apple Loops** (or "Drummer Loops") are a new addition in the 10.3.2 update.

## ⦿ Installation

- ☑ Logic v10.3.2 come with 444 new Apple Loops (157MB) that are stored in the same System Library as the other Apple Loops in a new subfolder named "*13 Drummer*" ❶ */Library/Audio/ Apple Loops/Apple/13 Drummer/*

- ☑ You can check in Logic's Sound Library Manager Window ❷ (Main Menu *Logic Pro X ➤ Sound Library ➤ Open Sound Library Manager...*) to see if the loops are installed. They are listed in a new category "*Drummer*" ❸. If not installed yet, just select the checkbox next to the Drummer and *click* the Install Button.

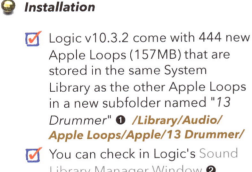

### Meet the new Drummer Loops

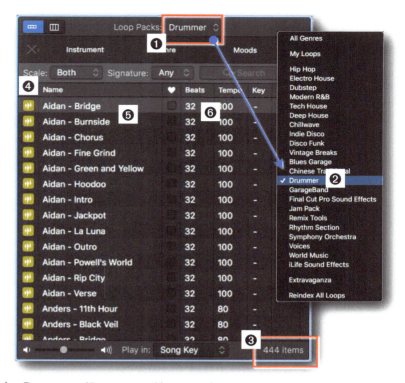

Once installed, all the new Drummer Loops are available in the Loop Browser together with the rest of the other installed Loops.

▶ **Loop Pack Drummer**: There is a quick way to display only the 444 new Drummer Loops by *clicking* on the Loop Packs Selector ❶ on top of the Loop Browser to open the Loop Packs Menu. You will see a new menu item "*Drummer*" ❷ that represents the newly installed folder "*13 Drummer*" folder we just saw, containing all the 444 Drummer Loops. The Status Bar indicates this number of 444 items ❸.

▶ **Drummer Loop Icon** 🟨 ❹: The Drummer Loops have their own yellow loop icon.

▶ **Name** ❺: The Drummer Loops all follow the same naming convention, indicating how the Drummer Loop was created. It starts with the name of the Drummer (Drummer Character) followed by the Drummer Preset that was used for that Loop. Please note that these are the same Drummer Presets that are available for that Drummer plus additional ones.

▶ **Beats** ❻: Each Drummer Loop is 8 bars long (32 beats).

▶ **Tempo**: The Tempo field indicates the original tempo the Loop was created in, but because they are Apple Loops, they adapt to the current Project Tempo.

### Search Drummer Loops

In addition to the Loop Pack selection "*Drummer*", you can use all the other search restrictions based on the Metadata Categories stored with the Drummer Loops. The available Category Buttons are active (dark).

▶ **Search Field** ❼: You can enter the name of a Drummer only to display his or her Loops, or search only for all "*Intros*" whatever is contained in the name.

▶ **Instrument** ❽: Narrow your search to Kits, Percussion, or specific Percussion Kit Pieces.

▶ **Genre** ❾: Narrow your search by specific music genres.

▶ **Moods** ❿: Narrow your search by these additional categories.

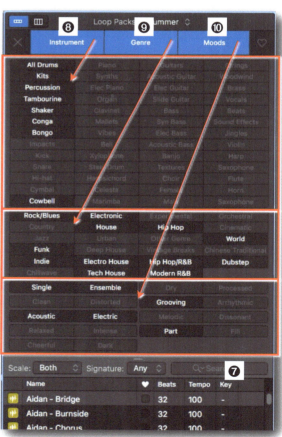

## 🍋 *What are Yellow Apple Loops*

So what are these yellow Drummer Loops and what can you use them for? To fully understand the functionality, you have to be aware of the concept of Apple Loops and the Drummer in general.

▸ A Drummer Loop originates from a Drummer Region ❶ (a specific Drummer Preset from a Drummer Character) played on a Drummer Track ❷.

▸ That specific Drummer Region is recorded/converted into a Yellow Apple Loop (Drummer Loop) as a CAF file ❸ (an audio file with the *.caf* file extension).

▸ The Drummer Loops CAF file contains the following data:

☑ **Drummer Region ❹**: This is the actual Drummer Region ❶ with its current play parameters during the conversion. Think of it as a stored Drummer Preset.

☑ **MIDI Region ❺**: A Drummer Region represents a drum pattern that produces MIDI Events sent to the sound module when played back. These MIDI Events are stored as a MIDI Region in the Drummer Loop. This is the similar procedure when you drag a Drummer Region onto the Track Lane of an Instrument Track. It also converts the Drummer Region into a MIDI Region.

☑ **Audio Region ❻**: This is like a bounce in-place procedure where a Drummer Region is bounced to an Audio Region ❶. This newly created audio file is time-based, so it can follow the tempo like other Apple Loops when imported to your Project.

☑ **Drummer ❼**: Remember, every Drummer Track has a specific Drummer assigned to it when you create that track, and its name is listed in parenthesis next to the Track Name. The name of the Drummer ❷ is also stored in the Drummer Loop.

☑ **Drummer Patch ❽**: Every Drummer uses a specific Drummer Patch with all the Channel Strip Settings. The name of this Drummer Patch is also included in the Drummer Loop.

☑ **Metadata ❾**: Like any other Apple Loop, the Drummer Loops also contains additional Metadata, i.e. the various Keywords like Instrument, Genre, Moods, or Tempo information.

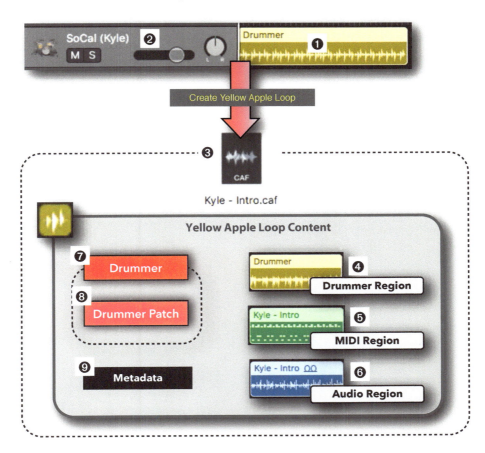

### 🌑 *How to use Drummer Loops*

Because of the rich content of a Drummer Loop, you have multiple options how to drag a Drummer Loop onto a Track Lane in the Workspace.

▶ **Empty Workspace**: *Drag* the yellow Drummer Loop to the empty Workspace (below the last Track):

- A new Drummer Track will be created loaded with the stored Drummer

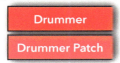

- The Stored Drummer Region will be placed on the Drummer Track

▶ **Drummer Track**: *Drag* the Drummer Loop onto a Drummer Track.

- If the Loop is based on the same Drummer as the Drummer Track you are dragging the Loop over, then the Drummer Region will be placed on that Track.

- If the Drummer Loop is based on a different Drummer but is the same type (DKD-based, DMD-based, or Percussion-based), then the Drummer Region from the Loop will be placed on that Track. However, you will get a warning message that the Loop may sound differently.

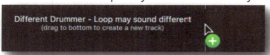

- If the Drummer Loop is based on a different type of Drummer (DKD-based, DMD-based, or Percussion-based), then you get a warning about that, and a new Drummer Track will be created with the Drummer and Drummer Region from the Loop.

▶ **Instrument Track**: *Drag* the Drummer Loop onto an Instrument Track.

- The MIDI Region will be placed on the Instrument Track, despite the fact that there is a warning on the Track Lane ("*Not a Drummer Track*").

- If there is no MIDI Region on the Track Lane yet, then the Drummer Patch will be loaded on that Track.

- If there is already a MIDI Region on the Track Lane, then the current Channel Strip Settings will not be overwritten. However, that MIDI Region doesn't make much sense if the current Instrument Plugin is not sample-mapped to that Drummer Loop.

▶ **Audio Track**: *Drag* the Drummer Loop onto an Audio Track.

- The Audio Region will be placed on the Track Lane despite the fact that there is a warning on the Track Lane ("*Not a Drummer Track*").

*Attention*: *Dragging* the first Apple Loop to an Instrument Track or Audio Track will adjust the Volume Fader on that Track to the current value of the Preview Volume Fader at the bottom of the Loop Browser.

### 🥁 *Create your own Drummer Loop*

Yes, you can create your own yellow Drummer Loop with the same procedure as creating blue or green Apple Loops. But why would you do that? Remember, when you create a new Drummer Track and edit your Drummer Regions, you configure the parameters in the Drummer Editor for that Drummer Region (the play instructions for the Drummer). You can save those settings as your custom Drummer Presets, but those are only available through the Drummer Editor when you have exactly that Drummer loaded on a Drummer Track.

Now when you create a Drummer Loop out of a Drummer Region, you have the following advantages:

▸ The Drummer Preset (the instructions) is available to any Drummer Track as long as it is the same type of Drummer (DKD-based, DMD-based, or Percussion-based).

▸ You can load that Drummer Preset in the form of a MIDI File to any Software Instrument to play those play instructions (stored as MIDI Events in that MIDI Regions) on any drummer plugin.

▸ You can load the audio file of the Drummer Loop onto any Audio Track to have a specific groove available as a simple Audio Region without the sometimes huge overhead of a Drummer Track. Because these are tempo-matched audio files, they follow your Project Tempo.

**Add Region to Apple Loops Library Dialog**

This is the procedure to create a Drummer Loop:

☑ Select the (single) Drummer Region in your Workspace that you want to convert into a Drummer Loop.

☑ If the Drummer Region is less than 8 bars long, then it will automatically be looped to 8 bars during the conversion.

☑ *General Tip*: If the Drummer Region starts before the downbeat, it will start with a pickup fill that will also be converted into the Drummer Loop.

☑ Choose from the Main Menu *File ➤ Export ➤ Region to Loop Library* or Key Command *sh+ctr+O* or *drag* the Region over to the Loop Browser.

☑ Set the name and the metadata for the loop in the Add Region to Apple Loops Library Dialog ❶.

☑ When *clicking* the Create Button ❷, you will see a window indicating the bouncing progress ❸.

☑ Logic will automatically re-index your Loop Library. You can quickly access your new Drummer Loop by selecting the "*My Loops*" ❹ option in the Loop Packs Menu ❺.

**Loop Browser**

## Toolbar

### Renamed Items in Toolbar Configuration Popover

The Toolbar Configuration Popover ❶ lists all the controls that you can show/hide on the Toolbar ❷. Five of the labels on this popover have been renamed:

▸ Edit Groups ➤➤➤ **Groups** ❸
▸ Toggle Groups ➤➤➤ **Group Clutch** ❸
▸ Strip Silence ➤➤➤ **Remove Silence** ❺
▸ Nudge ➤➤➤ **Nudge Value** ❻
▸ Lock SMPTE ➤➤➤ **Lock/Unlock SMPTE** ❼

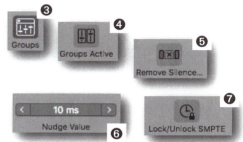

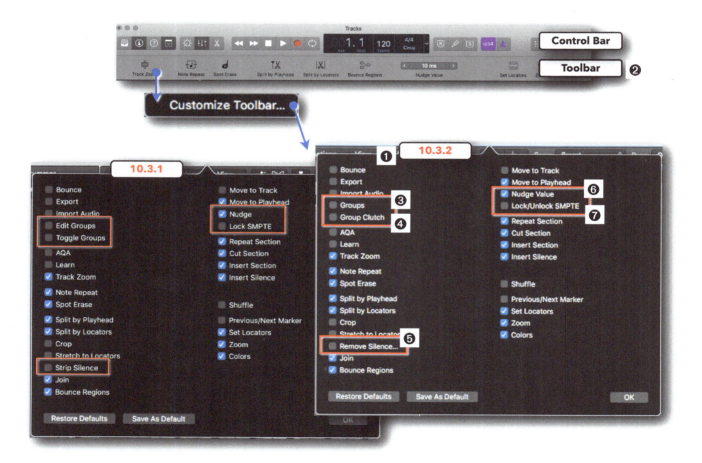

# Use Capture Recording for Smart Controls

 **Recap**

 Capture Recording is one of those features that will improve your workflow tremendously. Instead of hitting the Record Button first and then record your Track, you can play along with your Tracks in Play Mode and hit the "Capture Recording Button ❶ (or Key Command *sh+R*) while still playing or after you stop the playback. Whatever you played since you started the playback will appear as a new MIDI Region ❷ or whatever Overlapping MIDI Recording Mode you've selected. The Capture Recording Button is not displayed with the Transport Controls by default. Enable it from the Control Bar Configuration Popover.

<u>Attention</u>: Although Capture Recording is for MIDI Regions, it also can be used for recording audio. How often did it happen that the artist or the band started playing and you forgot to press the Record Button? Not anymore, I explain exactly how to pull this off in my book "<u>Logic Pro X - Tips, Tricks, Secrets #1</u>".

 **10.3.2**

The new additional functionality for the Capture Recording in v10.3.2 has to do with Smart Controls.

- ▶ You already could record any movement of the onscreen controllers in the Smart Controls ❸ together with your MIDI Event, and they are stored together in the MIDI Region ❷ as so-called Fader Events. Look for the Status Column in the Event List with the entry "Fader" ❹. The Length/Info Column ❺ displays the name of the corresponding controllers, where you can edit them like MIDI Events.

- ▶ Now, when you move those onscreen controls during playback, they are also recorded in a buffer together with the other MIDI Events so you can use the Capture Recording ❶ to recall those Fader Events into the MIDI Region without having pressed the Record Button.

- ▶ Please note that using Capture Recording could also "record" MIDI Regions on an Audio Track ❻ with those Smart Controls data as Fader Events. However, you might want to use the command *Track ➤ Others ➤ New Track with same Channel* (Key Command *sh+ctr+return*) to create a separate Track to have Audio Regions and MIDI Regions on different Track Lanes (but still playing through the same assigned Channel Strip).

**Control Bar**

## Additional Display Modes

➡️ *10.3.1*

The LCD ❶ in the Control Bar could be set to any of the five Display Modes ❷, depending on what elements you want to see on the LCD. *Click* the Display Mode Selector ❸, the little downward arrow on the right to open the Display Mode Menu with the five options ❷.

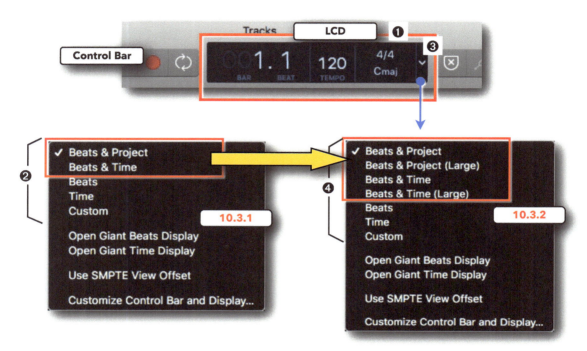

➡️ *10.3.2*

Now you have two additional Display Modes for a total of seven Display Modes ❹.

This is how the first four Display Modes have changed.

▸ **"Beats & Projects" ❺**: This is a new "compact" Display Mode without the Division and Ticks value and the Key Signature.

▸ **"Beats & Projects (Large)" ❻**: This Display Mode is the same as the 10.3.1 "Beats & Project, just with the position for the Time Signature and Key Signature swapped.

▸ **"Beats & Time" ❼**: This is a new "compact" Display Mode without the Division and Ticks values for the Beats information and without the Frames and Subframes for the Time information.

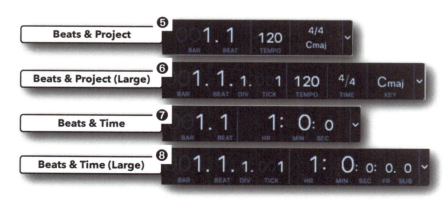

▸ **"Beats & Time" (Large)" ❽**: This Display Value is the same as the 10.3.1 "Beats & Time".

# Cycle Button Moved Next to the Transport Controls

The Cycle Button ❶ on the Control Bar has been moved to the Transport Controls ❷ next to the Record Button. The Key Signature and Time Signature elements have swapped position ❸.

# "Recording Preferences..." Command in Record Button Shortcut Menu

The Shortcut Menu that opens when you *ctr+click* on the Record Button ❹ now has an additional item, "Record Preferences..." ❺ to access the Record Preferences directly from that button.

Remember, a button on the Control Bar shows a little downward arrow when you move the cursor over it to indicate that it has a Shortcut Menu when you *ctr+click* on it. Don't confuse that with the little downward arrow on the LCD ❻ that opens a menu by just *clicking* on it.

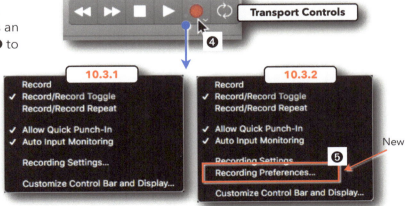

## Ruler

### Trimming/Moving Cycle Area doesn't cover Ruler Tracks anymore

When trimming or moving the Cycle Range, it is not possible anymore that the Help Tag Popover covers the Ruler Tracks ❶ when you move up the mouse vertically.

This improvement belongs to the "*Attention to Details*" category.

## Global Tracks

### Visually Overlapping Infinite Marker Tracks

➡️ *Recap*

When you create a new Marker, Logic creates a so-called Infinite Marker ❷, which means it doesn't have a specific end position. This is indicated in the Marker List with a Length value of 1 Tick ❸ (or 1 Frame). On the Marker Track, that Marker would stretch all the way to the end of your Project. However, if you create a second Marker after that, then the first Marker seems to end at the start position of that following Marker.

In that situation, it is not obvious anymore that the first Marker is an Infinite Marker.

➡️ *10.3.2*

Now, if an Infinite Marker is visually truncated on the Marker Track by a following Marker ❹, then that is indicated with that tiny overlap ❺ into the following Marker at the upper portion of the Marker Bar.

Please note that this could also indicate that the first Marker might be a Length-limited Marker, just ending after the start position of the following Marker.

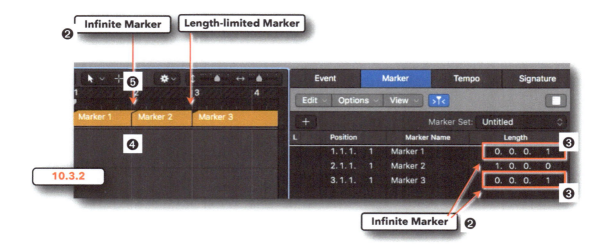

## Corrected Key Command for "Reset Individual Track Zoom"

The following is a correction of a "typo".

The Local View Menu in the Tracks Area listed a wrong Key Equivalent. Instead of the wrong **ctr+opt+cmd+ForwardDelete** ❶, it now displays the correct **ctr+opt+cmd+BackwardDelete** (the regular delete key) Key Equivalent ❷.

**Tracks Are: Local View Menu**

 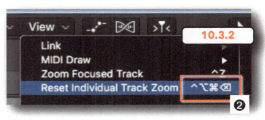

**Region Inspector**

## Region Transpose value is displayed in the Region Header

Any Transpose value applied in the Region Inspector ❸ will be displayed on the Region Header in parenthesis ❹. Changing the Transpose Value will show the changes on the Region Header in real time.

**Tracks Area**

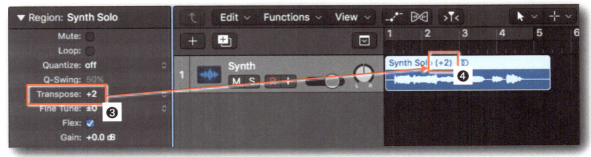

# New Transpose and Fine Tune Parameters

 **Recap**

The ability to transpose an Audio Region depends on where the audio file was created and what type of audio file it is. Logic differentiates between three types:

- ☑ Audio Files recorded in the current Project
- ☑ Apple Loops dragged onto the Audio Track
- ☑ Standard Audio Files imported to the Project

 **New**

Not only does the new version 10.3.2 add a new "Fine Tune" ❶ parameter in the Region Inspector (Region-based Tuning), but it also changes the behavior, what parameters are displayed and what algorithm is used. Pay close attention because there are a few little details that can be easily overlooked.

 **Record New Audio Region**

This is the behavior when you record new audio in a Project:

- ▶ **10.3.1**: After the recording, the Region Inspector displays the Follow Tempo & Pitch ❷ checkbox, but only if you enable the checkbox will the Transpose parameter be displayed above. The behavior is similar to Audio Loops. You can transpose the Audio Region, and its tempo will adjust if you change the Project Tempo.

- ▶ **10.3.2**: Be really careful what happens now in 10.3.2:
  - After the recording, the Region Inspector again displays the disabled Follow Tempo & Pitch checkbox
  - The Transpose ❹ parameter (-36 semitones ... +36 semitones) and the new Fine Tune ❺ parameter (-50 cent ... +50cent, 100cent = 1semitone) are displayed right away.
  - If you enable the Follow Tempo & Pitch ❸ checkbox first and change the Transpose or Fine Tune value, Logic will use the same procedure as in 10.3 (with the additional Fine Tune).
  - If you leave the Follow Tempo & Pitch checkbox disabled and change the Transpose or the Fine Tune value, the checkbox changes to the Flex checkbox ❻ and is automatically enabled.
  - Now Logic uses the much better Flex algorithms for transposition. You can change the Flex Algorithms manually (Polyphonic, Slice, etc.) in the Track Inspector.
  - The Flex checkbox will automatically disabled when you set the Transpose and Fine Tune values to 0. If you manually enabled the checkbox, it stays enabled even if you set the values to 0.
  - When you disable the Flex checkbox, any Transpose or Fine Tune value will be displayed in parenthesis ❼.
  - If you set Flex to off in the Track Inspector, the checkbox changes back to Follow Tempo & Pitch ❸.
  - Please note that, unlike Follow Tempo & Pitch, Flex Mode doesn't adjust to tempo changes, unless you have Follow Tempo & Pitch enabled before activating Flex Mode.

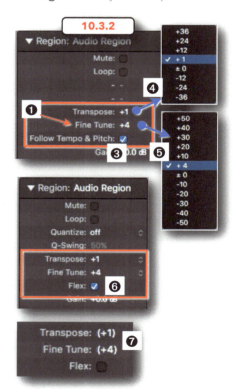

### 🧙 Imported Apple Loop

The following has changed when you *drag* an Apple Loop from the Loop Browser to the Track Lane:

‣ **10.3.1**: The Follow Tempo & Pitch checkbox ❶ is automatically enabled with the Transpose parameter visible.

‣ **10.3.2**: The Follow Tempo & Pitch checkbox is automatically enabled ❷, and in addition to the Transpose ❸ parameter, the Region Inspector now displays the new Fine Tune ❹ parameter.

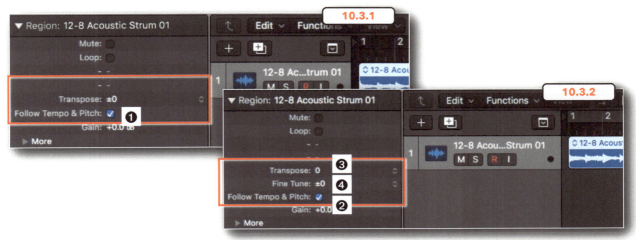

### 🧙 Imported Audio File

This has changed when you import/drag an audio file from the Finder to an Audio Track:

‣ **10.3.1**: No parameters ❺ are available in the Region Inspector to transpose the Audio Region.

‣ **10.3.2**: The Transpose ❻ and the new Fine Tune ❼ parameter are now available in the Region Inspector. Now you can transpose or tune an imported Audio Region right away, which was not possible in earlier versions! Once you set any of those parameter values ❽, Flex will be enabled on that Track. The Flex checkbox appears ❾ in the Region Inspector and is enabled. Remember you can select a different Flex Algorithm to optimize the results.

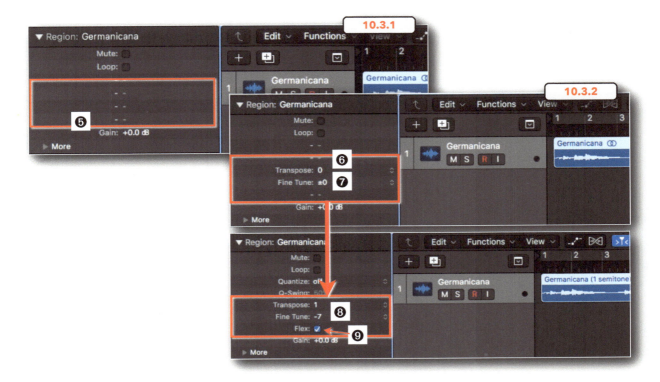

## Duplicate Track with Record Enable

Now when a Track is record-enabled (Record Enable Button blinking ❶) and you duplicate that Track, then the new Track will be record enabled ❷ instead of the original Track ❸.

This is very useful when you are recording on a Track, and next, want to record on a separate Track. You just use the Duplicate Track command (*cmd+D* or *click* on the Duplicate Track Button ❹ ), and you are ready to go without first disabling the Record Enable Button on the previous Track and enabling the Record Enable Button on the new Track.

Remember, *cmd+clicking* on the Duplicate Track Button will also duplicate all the Regions (and Automation) to the new Track.

## Show/Hide Inactive Track Alternatives on <u>All</u> Tracks

*Clicking* on the Track Alternatives Selector ❺ (the little double-arrow ⬍) will open the Track Alternatives Menu ❻ with the menu item *Sow/Hide Inactive* ❼.

Holding down the *option* key while selecting this command will now toggle all Tracks in your Project to show or hide their Inactive Track Alternatives.

This command is now also available as a Key Command *Show/Hide All Inactive Alternatives* ❽.

**Key Commands**

# Menu Items for Track Header Component rearranged

**Shortcut Menu**

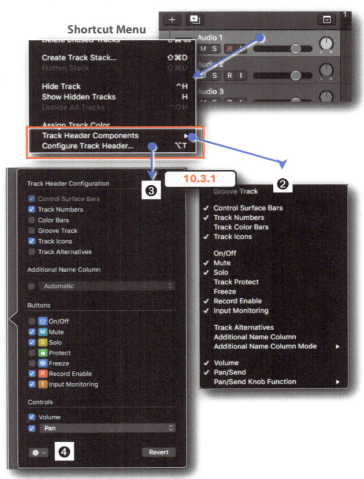

### ➡ *Recap*

Track Header Components ❶ are the elements that are displayed on the Track Header.

From two place you can choose which components you want to show or hide:

### 🔘 *Track Header Components Menu* ❷

The Track Header Components Menu is a submenu on the Track Header Shortcut Menu that lists all the components that you can select or deselect.

### 🔘 *Track Header Configuration Popover*

The Shortcut Menu has a second command that opens the Track Header Configuration Popover ❸, listing the same components (plus some view management controls under the Gear Button ❹). This popover is more convenient because it lets you configure what you want while the window stays opens. Also, the Track Header updates right away when you make changes.

### ➡ *10.3.2*

The components on the popover ❺ and submenu ❻ have been re-arranged in a more "logical" way, and also, the order of the components now is the same on the popover and submenu, which was not the case in 10.3.1.

The Gear Button has been moved next to the "Revert" Button ❼.

BTW, the order of the buttons and control from left to right on the Track Header reflects the order on the menu and popover.

# Updated Track Icons

There are a few small changes and additions to the Track Icons. **Ctr-click** the Track Icon on the Track Header to open the Track Icon Popover.

 *Percussion*

Two new icons ❶ ❷

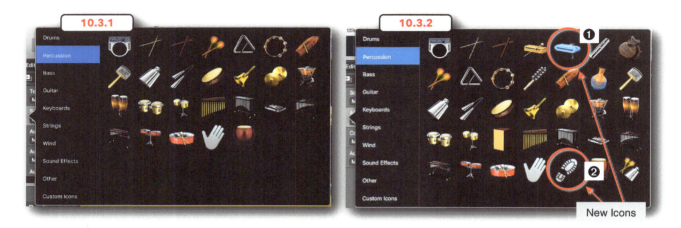

 *Strings*

Different font ❸

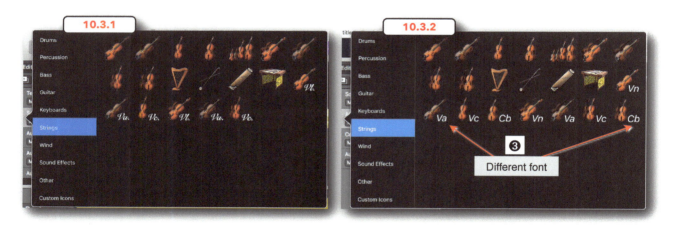

 *Wind*

Different font ❹

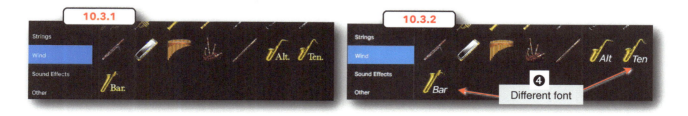

# Drummer Character Name displayed with the Track Name

The Drummer Track displays the name of the Drummer Character ❶ in parenthesis after the Track Name. This is a nice way to spot a Drummer Track in your Project (unless you use a naming convention that involves putting names in parenthesis). The Drummer Name disappears when you edit the Track Name with your own custom name, however, deleting your custom name, will display the original Path Name again with the Drummer Character in parenthesis.

Please pay attention to the Track Icon that indicates if this Drummer is based on the Drum Kit Designer ❷ ("DKD-based"), the Drum Machine Designer ❸ ("DMD-based"), or the EXS24 ❹ (Percussion-based).

# Changes on Shortcut Menu for the Track Header

*Ctr+clicking* on a Track Header opens its Shortcut Menu ❺. There are two minor changes on the first and last menu item:

- ▶ **Current Channel Strip**: In 10.3.1, the first item on the menu listed the name of the Channel Strip ❻ that is assigned to that Track. Now in 10.3.2, that menu item is no longer displayed.
- ▶ **Configure Track Header**: This menu command now has the added dots (...) ❼ to indicate the command opens a window.

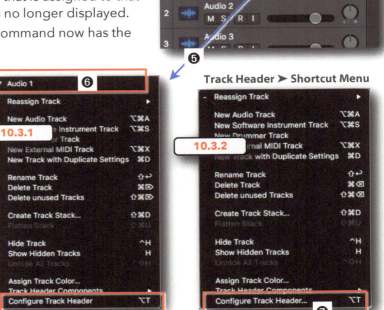

## Vertical Crosshair Line for Loop Trimming

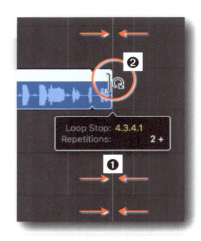

Logic displays a vertical crosshair line when trimming the borders of a Region or when moving a Region. Now in 10.3.2, it also displays a crosshair line ❶ when trimming a looped Region ❷.

## Plus Button ⊕ at the right border of Drummer Regions

➡ *10.3.1*

To create a new Drummer Region on a Drummer Track, you either *click* with the Pencil Tool ✎ on the Track or *ctr+click* on the Track Lane ❸ and choose from the *Shortcut Menu ➤ Create Drummer Region* ❹.

➡ *10.3.2*

Now you have an additional option. When you move the mouse cursor close to the right border ❺ of a Drummer Region at an area where there is no Drummer Region or the beginning of the (empty) Track Lane ❻, a yellow "plus" button ⊕ appears at the Region border. *Click* on it, and a new Drummer Region will be created 8 bars long or with the length to fill any gap between two Drummer Region if it is less than 8 bars.

If you don't like that feature, you can disable it with a checkbox ❼ in the *Preferences ➤ Display ➤ Tracks ➤ Regions ➤ "Show "+" Button next to Drummer Regions*.

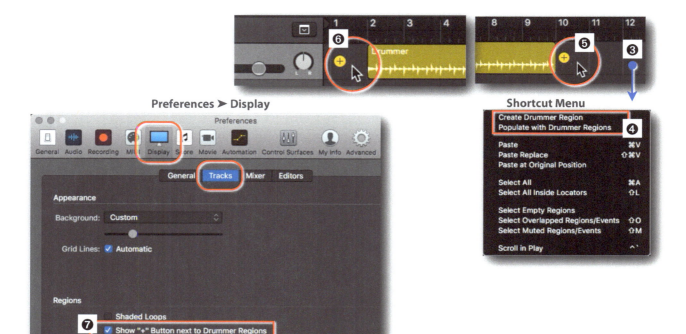

## Plus Button ⊕ Behavior

When you create a new Drummer Region by using the "*Create Drummer Region*" command from the Shortcut Menu (*ctr+click* on an empty Drummer Track Lane) or using the Pencil Tool ✎, then Logic loads the Default Drummer Preset of the current Drummer for that Drummer Region.

Using the yellow Plus Button ⊕ also creates a new Drummer Region, but not necessarily based on the Default Drummer Preset:

- ▶ If the +Buttons appears at the right border of a Drummer Region ❶, then the newly created Drummer Region will inherit the same parameters of that previous Drummer Region

- ▶ If the +Button appears on an empty space at the beginning of that Track ❷, then the newly created Drummer Region will be based on the Default Drummer Preset.

- ▶ If you have any Arrangement Markers ❸ (Global Tracks) defined along that Timeline where you want to create the new Drummer Region, then the new Drummer Preset uses the Preset with the same name as the Arrangement Marker (Intro, Outro, Verse, etc.). These Presets are also located in the individual Presets folder on the hard drive

but will not be loaded (visible) into the Beat Presets List in the Drummer Editor. I cover all those details about that behavior, especially with the Arrangement Markers in my book "Logic Pro X - How it Works"

## Bounce In Place (BiP) Drummer Summing Stacks

Now it is possible to use the "*Bounce in Place*" command on Drummer Tracks that use Summing Stacks. Use any of the two commands:

- 📌 *Ctr+click* on the Drummer Track and select from the ***Shortcut Menu ➤ Bounce and Join ➤ Bounce in Place*** ❹
- 📌 Key Command *ctr+B*

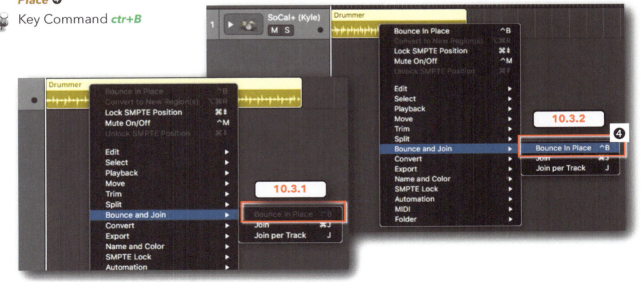

## Bounce In Place (BiP) Drummer Summing Stacks

If you have a Software Instrument (i.e. Ultrabeat ) with multiple audio outputs routed to individual Aux Channel Strips ❷ and use their corresponding Aux Tracks ❸ to record the MIDI Regions ❹ on them, then you can now use the "Bounce in Place" ❺ command on those MIDI Region located on Aux Tracks.

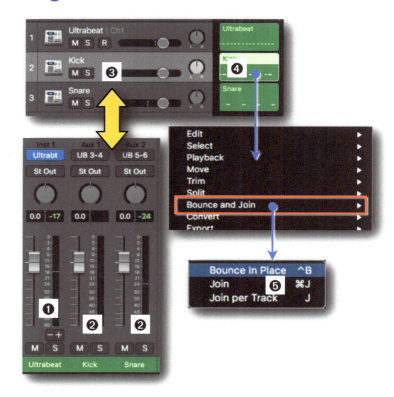

The Bounce in Place command is available as:

- 🎚 Key Command *ctr+B*
- 🎚 Main Menu *File ➤ Bounce ➤ Regions in Place*
- 🎚 *Right-click* on the Region and select from the *Shortcut Menu➤ Bounce and Join ➤ Bounce in Place* ❺

## Trim Region Start/End to Previous/Next Region as Menu Commands

The two Key Commands ❻ "*Trim Region Start to Previous Region*" and "*Trim Region End to Next Region*" are now also available as menu commands:

- ▶ From the Main Main Menu *Edit ➤ Trim ➤*
- ▶ *Ctr+clicking* on a Region and selecting from the *Shortcut Menu ➤ Trim ➤*.

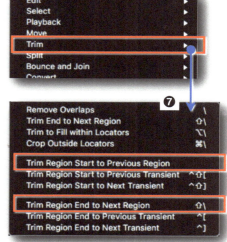

# Opt+drag Plugins in Selection-Based Processing Window

The behavior has changed when *opt+dragging* ❶ a Plugin between Plugin Set A and Plugin Set B:

▶ **10.3.1**: When you *opt+drag* a Plugin over an existing Plugin on the other Plugin Set, the existing Plugin will be moved down one slot ❷ to make space for the Plugin that you drag over ❸.

▶ **10.3.2**: When you *opt+drag* a Plugin over an existing Plugin on the other Plugin Set, then the existing Plugin on that Slot will be replaced ❹ with the Plugin that you drag over.

**Selection-Based Processing Window**

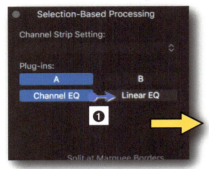

# Trimming the Start of an Alias MIDI Regions converts it to Real Copy

*Opt+dragging* a MIDI Region creates an independent copy of that Region. *Sh+opt+dragging* creates an Alias of that MIDI Region ❺, which is handy if you want to stack Software Instrument sounds on multiple Tracks. This only requires editing the one Region. All its Alias Regions play accordingly.

You can trim the right border of an Alias Region, but not the left border anymore (which caused timing/sync problems). Now, when you trim the left border ❻ of an Alias MIDI Region, Logic automatically converts it to a real copy, an independent MIDI Region.

This is the same procedure as converting an Alias MIDI Region into a Real Copy, by *double-clicking* on the Region and pressing "Real Copy" button on the Dialog Window.

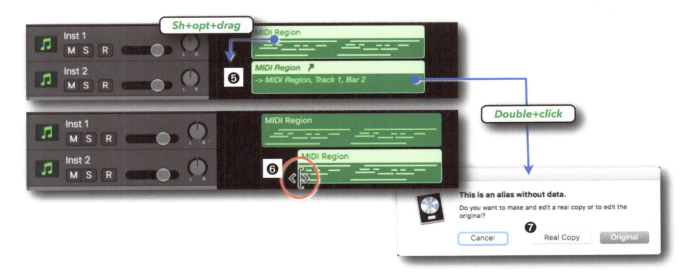

## Select Tracks on Region Selection

This is a new feature I was waiting for like, forever.

You always could choose a preference that, when selecting a Track, all the Regions on that Track would automatically be selected ("*Select regions on track selection*" ❶). However, it didn't work the other way around that when you select a Region in the Workspace it would automatically select the Track it is placed on. But now it does.

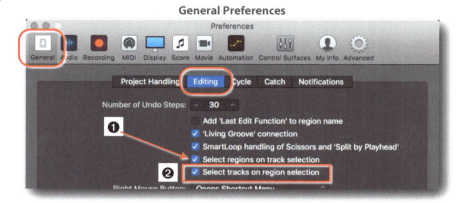

**General Preferences**

The checkbox "**Select tracks on region selection**" ❷ in the *Preferences* ➤ *General* ➤ *Editing* has finally arrived.

Please note that Logic already has a Key Command "*Select Track by Region/Folder*" that lets you manually select the Track of a selected Region (the first Track is multiple Regions on multiple Tracks are selected). Now with this new Preference, it does it automatically.

## Renamed Fade Out Command

 *Recap*

There is a strange command in the Main Menu *Mix* ➤ *Create Track Automation* ➤ *Fade Out* ❸ that many Logic users might have never used. It is a feature from GarageBand that automatically creates a 10-second Fade Out ❹ on the Output Channel Strip by creating four Control Points on that Track. It will be on the Output Channel Strip if you have a stereo Project or on the Master Channel Strip if you have a surround Project.

 *10.3.2*

That "*Fade Out*" ❺ command has been renamed to "*Create Volume Fade Out on Main Output*" ❺, including the corresponding renaming for the Key Command (show of hands, how many have ever used that Key Command?)

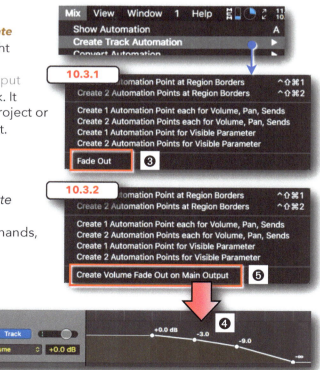

## Rename Active Track Alternative

Now you can **_double-click_** the name of the Active Track Alternative ❶ on the Track Header to get a text field to enter a new name for that Track Alternative. In 10.3.1, a double-click opened a text field to rename the Track Name.

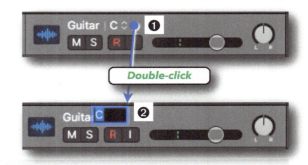

## Track Alternative Shortcut Menu

The following is a correction of a misplaced Key Command.

 ### _10.3.1_

When you **_ctr+click_** on the Track Header of an Inactive Track Alternative, a Shortcut Menu ❸ opens with two commands to rename or to delete that Inactive Track Alternative. So these two commands only affect the Inactive Track Alternative that you ctr+clicked. The listed Key Equivalent on that menu **_ctr+alt+cmd+return_** ❹ is incorrect because this Key Equivalent ❺ lets you rename the Active Track Alternative on the Track Header and not the Inactive Track Alternative.

### _10.3.2_

The wrong Key Equivalent has been removed from the Shortcut Menu ❻, so everything is fine now. No big deal, but at least we reviewed the different rename commands and from now on pay attention to which Track Alternative you are about to rename, the Active Track Alternative or one of the Inactive Track Alternatives.

## Show/Hide Inactive Track Alternative on <u>All</u> Tracks

**_Clicking_** on the Track Alternative Selector ❼ (the little double-arrow) will open the Track Alternative Menu ❽ with the menu item **_Sow/Hide Inactive_** ❾. Holding down the **_option_** key while selecting this command will now toggle all Tracks in your Project to show or hide their Track Alternatives.

## Piano Roll Editor

## Drums Names in Note Labels

The Local View Menu ❶ in the Piano Roll Editor has two modes that have changed slightly, Drum Names and Note Labels ❷.

🔶 *Drum Names*

▶ **10.3.1**: When that option was enabled, the upright keyboard extended to the right to displays the name ❸ of any drum sample that is assigned to each specific key.

▶ **10.3.2**: Now, the Drum Names are automatically displayed when they are embedded in the Software Instrument. These could be the Patches/Instrument for the Drum Kit Designer, Ultrabeat, or some of the EXS24 Instruments (*Orchestral Kit* Patch), including all the new EXS Instruments used by the Percussion Drummer. When selecting the Drum Names option, the only thing that happens is that the upright keyboard changes to display Note Names ❹.

🔶 *Note Labels*

▶ **10.3.1**: The Note Bars in the Piano Roll show a Velocity Line ❺ that indicate the Velocity Value of that MIDI Note, its length in relation to the length of the Note Bar. If Note Labels is enabled in the View Menu ❷, the Note Bar displays the Note Name ❻ (Pitch) and the Velocity Value as a numeric value. You have to zoom in horizontally and vertically to a specific zoom level to display those labels.

▶ **10.3.2**: Now, when the MIDI Region is placed on a Track with a Software Instrument that contains Drum Names, then enabling the Note Labels will display the Drum Name ❼ and the Velocity Value on the Note Bars.

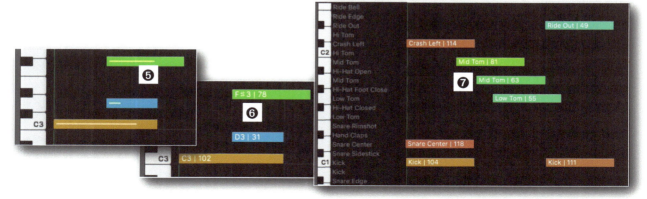

## Mute Column displays "M" instead of a Dot

There is a little cosmetic change in the Event List.

▶ **Mute Column**: The Mute Column now displays an *M* ❶ instead of a dot ❷ for any Event or Region that is muted.

▶ **Lock Column**: The Lock Column still displays the padlock, but it is now a simpler flat design ❸.

## Display Meta Event Name in Info Column

10.3.1 didn't display the name ❹ of Meta Events in the Info Column. Now it does ❺.

## "Increase/Decrease Last Clicked Parameter by 10" for MIDI Notes

There are two very handy Key Commands ❶ that let you quickly increase (*sh+equal*) or decrease (*sh+minus*) the parameter that you last clicked on (or dragged). That works on most of the on-screens controls (Volume, Pan, Sends, etc.) and also MIDI Events in the various MIDI Editors.

Now in 10.3.2, when you use the Key Command on a MIDI Note in the Event List (or other MIDI Editors), it transposes the MIDI Note by a value of 12 and not 10, which makes more sense musically.

Of course, you also have the dedicated Key Commands for transposing MIDI Notes ❷.

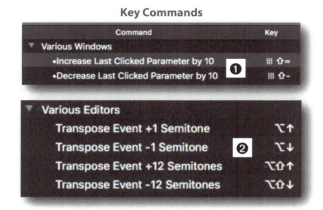

Key Commands

| Command | Key |
|---|---|
| **▼ Various Windows** | |
| •Increase Last Clicked Parameter by 10 | ⌗ ⇧= ❶ |
| •Decrease Last Clicked Parameter by 10 | ⌗ ⇧- |
| **▼ Various Editors** | |
| Transpose Event +1 Semitone | ⌥↑ |
| Transpose Event -1 Semitone | ⌥↓ ❷ |
| Transpose Event +12 Semitones | ⌥⇧↑ |
| Transpose Event -12 Semitones | ⌥⇧↓ |

## Global Edits

## New Key Command "Copy Section Between Locators (Global)"

Logic always had these special Section commands *Cut - Insert - Repeat* ❸, that let you define a section by the Locators (Cycle Range ❹) and apply those commands to that section. There are also two variations of those commands to apply it only to the Regions (Selection) or to the Regions and the Global Tracks (Global).

Now, 10.3.2 added a new Key Command "*Copy Section Between Locators (Global)*" ❺ that let you copy everything within the yellow Cycle Range borders, Regions ❻ and Global Track data ❼ so you can place them anywhere else along the timeline of your Project.

After initiating the command, a Dialog ❽ opens up first that might be a little bit confusing. "Move" ❾ means if you want to include the Global Track data.

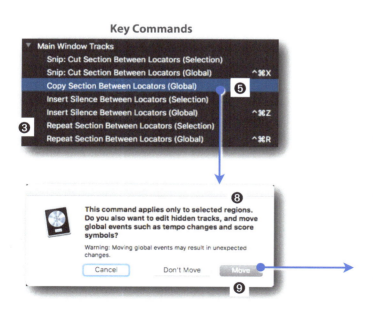

Key Commands

| **▼ Main Window Tracks** | |
|---|---|
| Snip: Cut Section Between Locators (Selection) | |
| Snip: Cut Section Between Locators (Global) | ⌃⌘X |
| Copy Section Between Locators (Global) ❺ | |
| Insert Silence Between Locators (Selection) | |
| Insert Silence Between Locators (Global) | ⌃⌘Z |
| Repeat Section Between Locators (Selection) | |
| Repeat Section Between Locators (Global) | ⌃⌘R |

❸

❽ This command applies only to selected regions. Do you also want to edit hidden tracks, and move global events such as tempo changes and score symbols?

Warning: Moving global events may result in unexpected changes.

Cancel    Don't Move    Move

❾

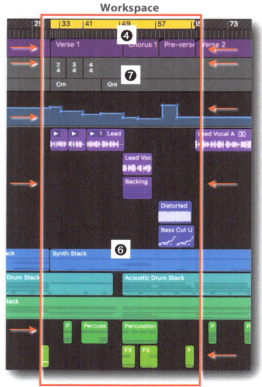

Workspace

## New Icons for Scene Markers in Lock Column

The Lock Column ❶ in the Marker List can indicate if a Marker is either locked or if it is a Scene Marker. Both icons have changed.

  ▶ **Scene Marker**: The icon has changed from "whatever that is supposed to be" icon ❷ to a clock icon ❸.
  ▶ **Locked Standard Marker**: The padlock icon ❺ has changed to a flat design padlock.

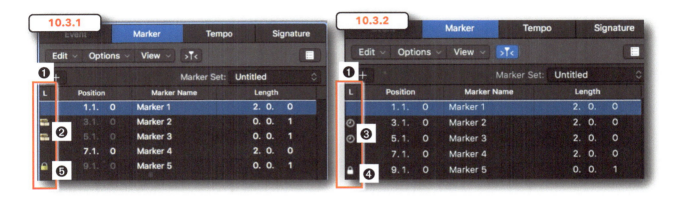

In case you wonder why the icon for the Scene Marker is also placed in the Lock Column, have a look at the Marker Track ❻, and you will know why. Scene Markers are automatically SMPTE-locked. That's why the SMPTE Lock icon is also displayed for Scene Markers ❼.

## Select Markers with Cmd+Click

Now you can *cmd+click* on individual Markers ❽ in the Marker List, and they will also be select in the Marker Track ❾ (didn't do that in 10.3.1).

However, when you *sh+click* on Markers to select an entire section, then they will be selected in the Marker List, but not on the Marker Track (room for improvement in the update 10.3.3 ?)

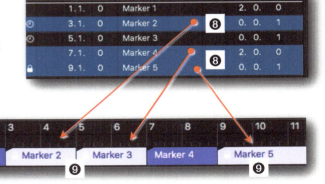

## Display Markers in the Linear View Mode

The Linear View Mode ❶  in the Score Editor now shows any Markers in the Ruler even when the Global Tracks are hidden ❸.

## Key Command "Toggle View" includes all Views

This is a small bug fix. When using the Key Command "*Toggle View*" ❹ it previously only toggled between Linear View and Wrapped View, now it steps through all three View Modes ❺ Linear View, Wrapped View, and Page View.

**Flex Pitch**

## New "Reset All" Command

In Flex Pitch Mode, when *ctr+clicking* on a Note Bar, the Shortcut Menu now has a new command "**Reset All**" ❻, which resets all Flex parameters of the currently selected Note Bars.

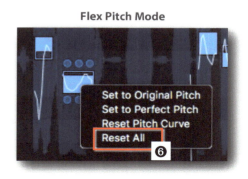

## Mixer

## Audio Device Controls for Stereo Tracks

 **Recap**

The Audio Device Controls ❶, the Channel Strip Components at the very top of an Audio Channel Strip, function as a remote control for the connected Audio Device (if it supports that feature). It lets you adjust the input gain of the Audio Device directly from Logic's Channel Strip.

 **10.3.2**

In 10.3.1, the Audio Device Controls only supported mono channel strips, but now in 10.3.2, they will also be displayed when the Channel Format ❷ is set to stereo.

## Solo-Safe remains on a solo/un-soloed Track

 **Recap**

**Ctr+clicking** on a Solo Button (Track Header or Channel Strip) toggles Solo Safe Mode for that Track. Solo Safe is indicated with a red line across the Solo Button ❸ 𝓢. Those solo-safe'd Tracks are not muted when a Solo is enabled on any other Track.

 **10.3.1**

If a Track is Solo Safe ❸ 𝓢 and you *click* on the Solo Button to solo that Track, the button switches to the standard Solo Mode ❹ S. When you *click* again to un-solo that Track, it should go back to its Solo Safe Mode state. This worked on the Channel Strip Solo Button, but not on the Track Header Solo Button. Now it works as expected on both. Also, when clicking the Solo Button of a solo-safe'd Channel Strip, in 10.3.1 it turned the Solo Button on its corresponding Track Header to this strange yellow button with the red line 𝓢. Not anymore. Now it displays the standard Solo Button S.

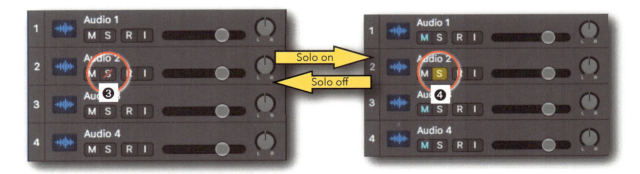

# Restrict Automatic Bus Assignment to higher Bus Numbers

## ➡️ *Recap*

Unlike a Channel Strip Setting that stores the complete configuration of a single Channel Strip, a Patch, on the other hand, can store additional routing information. That means when you load up a Patch, it could create a Channel Strip and additional Aux Channel Strips with Aux Sends on the Channel Strip routing the signal via Busses to those Aux Channel Strips. If you load a DMD-based Drummer Patch (Drum Machine Designer), Logic could load over 30 Channel Strips and use 10 Busses for various routing configurations. Logic automatically assigns those busses, using the next available (unused) Bus.

## ➡️ *10.3.2*

When you use Busses for your own routing purposes and, also, have a few of those Patches loaded that automatically assign Busses, then the Bus assignment looks a little bit unorganized and messy. It is especially annoying if you've set up Custom Labels for your Busses (Reverb, Delay, Drum Group, etc.) in the I/O Labels Window and the automatic Buss assignment of a Drummer uses those "labeled" Busses.

To avoid that potential mess, 10.3.2 now has a new Preferences setting in the **Preferences ➤ Audio ➤ General** "*Automatic Bus Assignment uses*" ❶ that forces Logic to only use Busses above a specific Bus Number ❷ when automatically assign Busses. That leaves a specific range of Busses for you to manually assign.

Here are two examples:

### 🔵 *All Busses*

"All busses" ❸ means no restrictions and the two DMD Instruments (using a lot of Busses) occupy the busses starting with Bus 1 ❺.

### 🔵 *Busses above 8*

When setting the restriction "*Busses above 8*" ❺, you can see the same Busses used by the two DMD Instruments, now starting at Bus 9 ❻. Bus 1 to Bus 8 is not used yet ❼.

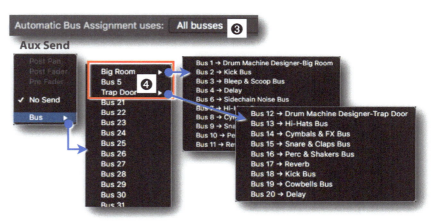

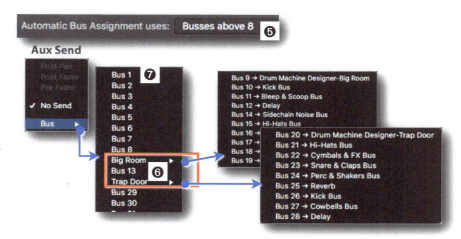

## Drag Pan Position And Pan Spread on the Pan Control

The Pan Control on a Stereo Channel Strip can be set to a true Stereo Pan by
***ctr+clicking*** on the Pan Control and selecting from the ***Shortcut Menu ➤ Stereo Pan***
❶. Now you have to pay attention where you move the mouse cursor over or click
on to know what parameter you are adjusting: Here is a review of the functionality
with the note from the release notes:

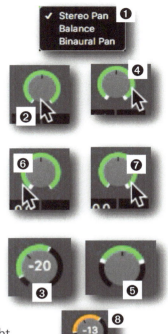

▶ **Center**: Moving the mouse cursor over the center ❷ affects the Pan
Position. ***Dragging*** the cursor up/down will change the Pan Position ❸.

▶ **Ring**: Moving the mouse cursor over the ring ❹ will highlight the two
white handles on each side of the ring. ***Dragging*** the cursor up/down will
change the Pan Spread ❺. The release note says: "*It is now possible to
adjust either the pan or spread position of a Stereo Panner using a mouse
or swipe gesture on a Magic Mouse, or two-finger swipe on a track pad*".

▶ **Left Handle**: Moving the mouse cursor over the left handle ❻ will
highlight only that handle. ***Dragging*** the cursor up/down will change the
Pan Spread by adjusting the left corner.

▶ **Right Handle**: Moving the mouse cursor over the right handle ❼ will
highlight only that handle. ***Dragging*** the cursor up/down will change the
Pan Spread by adjusting the right corner.

▶ **Swap Left-Right**: Don't forget the ***cmd+click*** on the ring to swap the left-right
channel, indicated by an orange ring ❽.

## Output Selection on New Tracks Dialog displays Custom Labels

The I/O Labels Window (Main Menu ***Mix ➤I/O
Labels...***) lets you assign custom labels ❾ to
the Hardware Inputs, Hardware Output, and
Busses.

Now the Output Selector ❿ in the New Tracks
Dialog (***opt+cmd+N***) also displays those
Custom Labels in parenthesis on the selector
and the popup menu. And yes, you can use
emojis.

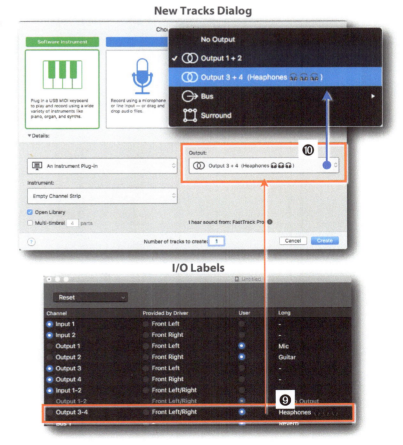

New Tracks Dialog

I/O Labels

## Tuner Button on Smart Controls Window for Audio Tracks

The Smart Controls Window for an Audio Track now has a Tuner Button ❶ on the far-right of its menu bar that toggle the Tuner Window ❷ on and off. This button has the same functionality as the Tuner Button ❸ on the Control Bar.

Smart Controls Window

Control Bar

Tuner Window

## Amp Designer and Pedalboard Button on Smart Controls Window

The Smart Controls Window for an Audio Track displays an Amp Designer Button ❹ and Pedalboard Button ❺ on the far-right of the menu bar if they are loaded as Audio FX Plugin on that Track. They toggle their Amp Designer Plugin Window ❻ and Pedalboard Plugin Window ❼ on/off.

Smart Controls Window

Amp Designer Plugin

Pedalboard Plugin

## Bounce Dialog

When you use the "*Bounce Region In Place*" command, the Bounce Regions In Place Dialog opens.

Now the "*Include Audio Tail in File*" checkbox ❶ stays active (so you can check or uncheck it) when "*Bypass Effects Plugin-Ins*" is disabled ❷.

**Bounce Regions in Place Dialog**

Bounce Regions In Place

Name: Drums

Destination: ○ New Track
　　　　　　 ○ Selected Track

Source: ○ Leave
　　　　 ● Mute
　　　　 ○ Delete

　　　　 Include Instrument Multi-Outputs
❷　　 ☐ Bypass Effect Plug-ins
❶　　 ☑ Include Audio Tail in File
　　　　☐ Include Audio Tail in Region
　　　　☑ Include Volume/Pan Automation

Normalize: Overload Protection Only

Restore Defaults　　　　Cancel　　OK

**Plugins**

## Linked Dual Mono Mode ("Couple")

 **Recap**

Logic 10.3 introduced the Dual Mono Mode for Plugins. That means, on a Stereo Channel Strip, a single inserted Plugin loads two independent Plugins, one for the left and one for the right channel. They can be set independently on the Plugin Window by *clicking* on the "L" Button ❸ or "R" Button ❹ to access the Plugin for the left channel or right channel.

**Plugin Window**

Audio 1
Factory Default　　　Side Chain: None
< >　Compare　Copy　Paste　　View: 52%
　　⚙ L R Couple
❸ ❹

Audio 1
Factory Default　　　Side Chain: None
< >　Compare　Copy　Paste　　View: 52%
　　⚙ L R Couple ❺

 **New "Couple" button**

When enabled, the new "Couple" Button ❺ next to the "L" Button and "R" Button links the controls of those two channels (left and right) of a Dual Mono Plugin instance or all the instances of a Multi Mono Plugin (surround). Please pay attention to the detail:

The left and right channel of the Track is still processed by two independent mono instances of that Plugin. When you enable the "Couple" Button, any control on the left channel Plugin that you adjust will be set to the same value on the right channel Plugin and vice versa. Any other controls that you don't touch keep their independent values. Disabling the "Couple" Button lets you control the parameters independently again.

This is convenient if you quickly want a specific control set to the same value on the left and right Plugin.

## Configuration Button now is the Gear Button

The Configuration Button ❶ on a Dual Mono Plugin has changed to a Gear Button ❷. The functionality is the same; it switches the Plugin Window to show the controls for bypassing ❸ individual channels plus a few other controls. They are especially useful for Multi-Mono Plugins ("Dual Mono" equivalent for Surround).

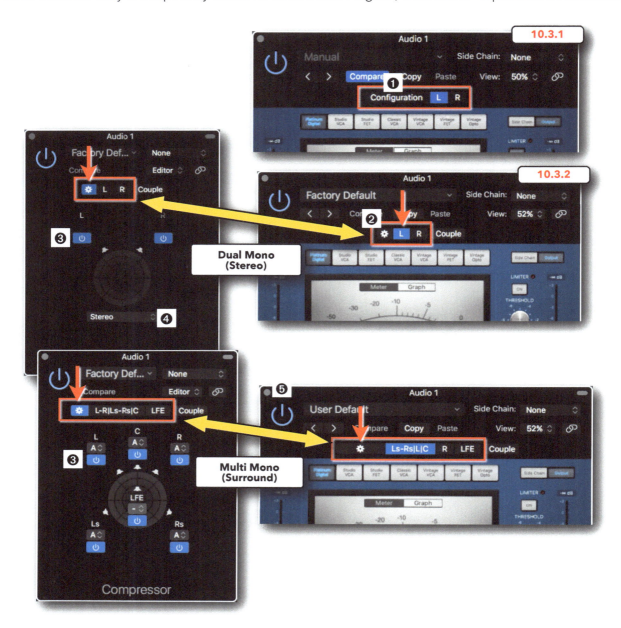

## Bypass individual Plugin Channels (fixed)

The Bypass Buttons in the Configuration View ❸ of the Plugin now work as expected. Disabling the Power Button of one channel will only bypass that channel without affecting the other channel.

Disabling the Main Power Button ❺ on the upper-left corner of the Plugin Window bypasses all channels of the Plugins.

# Toggle "Recent Plugins" Functionality in Plugin Menu

 ***Recap***

Logic Pro X v10.3 introduced a new feature for the Audio FX Plugin Menu and the Instrument Plugin Menu. A section on top of those menus labeled "*Recent*" ❶ shows the last five loaded Plugins.

 ***10.3.2***

Some Logic users must have complaints about that feature because now there is a checkbox in the *Preferences ➤ Display ➤ Mixer* ❷ that lets you disable it.

Please note that you still have the option to place any often-used Plugin on top of the Plugin Window ❸ (below the Recent section). In the Plug-In Manager (Main Menu *Logic Pro X ➤ Preferences ➤ Plug-In Manager...*) *drag* that Plugin over the "*Top Level*" ❹ item on top of the Sidebar.

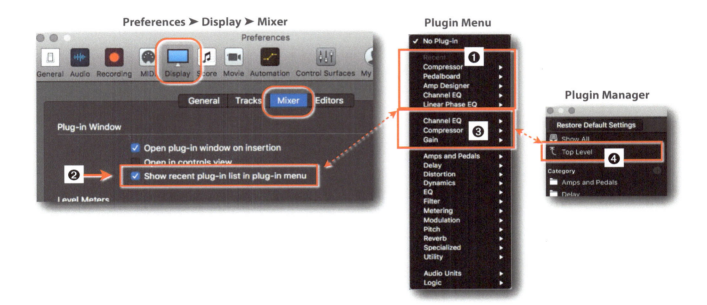

# Shift+click to close all Plugin Windows

There is a new handy click action to close all currently open Plugin Windows. *Sh+click* on the Close Button ❺ in the upper-left corner of any Plugin Window.

This is different from the *Hide All Plug-in Windows* command, which is the same function as the Key Command *V* or Main Menu *Window ➤ Hide All Plug-in Windows* ❻.

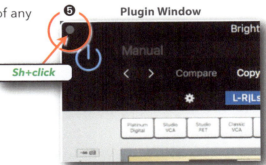

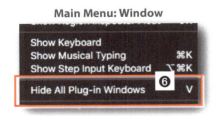

## Correlation Meter Reaction Time

The Correlation Meter Plugin (located in the Meter Category of the FX Plugins of a stereo Track) now has a Reaction Time selector.

***Click*** on the disclosure triangle to reveal the Reaction Selector ❶ that opens a popup menu with three options ❷ *Slow*, *Medium*, and *Fast*.

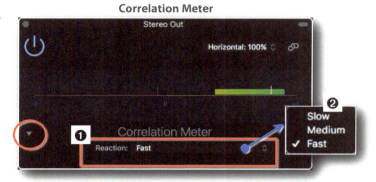

## Surround Panner new GUI

The Surround Panner has finally got its facelift:

▶ You open the Surround Panner when you ***double-click*** on the Pan Control ❸ of a Channel Strip.

▶ The disclosure triangle ❹ at the bottom has disappeared, and the three Separation parameters ❺ that were located in that area are now visible directly on the window with an additional Power Button ⏻ to toggle them on/off.

▶ Please note that there are two types of Panner, the Surround Panner and the Surround Balancer that automatically open when the Channel Format on the Channel Strip is mono or stereo ❻ (Surround Panner ❼) or surround ❽ (Surround Balancer ❾). I explain all those details in the Surround chapter of my book "Logic Pro X - The Details"

## Only one Drummer Region as Default

When creating a new Drummer Track (***Track ➤New Drummer Track***), Logic now only creates a single 8-bar Drummer Region ❶ instead of two Drummer Regions ❷.

## Empty Drummer Editor

Whenever you create a Drummer Track, Logic automatically creates a Default Drummer Regions that is selected, so the Drummer Editor in the Editors Pane at the bottom of Logic's Main Window displays its parameters.

However, if you select a Drummer Track that has no Drummer Region ❸ on its Track Lane (maybe you deleted them), then the Drummer Editor ❹ is blank. 10.3.2 added a little thing to that blank window, the yellow Plus Button ➕ ❺. *Click* on it to create a new Drummer Region on that Track at the beginning of the Project (regardless of the Playhead Position). This is the same button ➕ that now appears when you move the mouse cursor at the beginning of the Track Lane of the Drummer Track ❻ or close to the border of a Drummer Region (if that feature is not disabled in the ***Preferences ➤ Display ➤ Tracks ➤ Regions***).

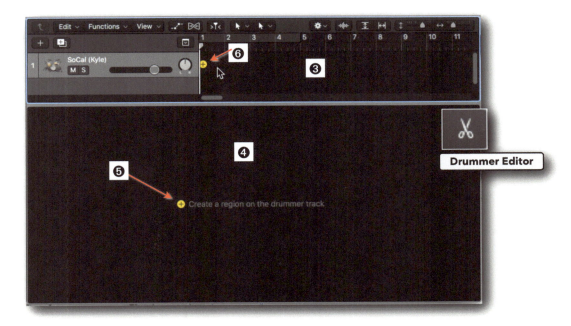

# Switch between a Basic Kit and Producer Kit+

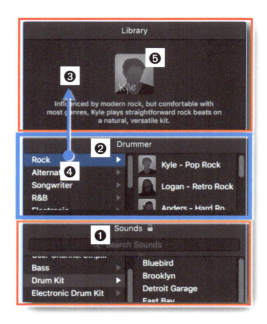

 ***Recap***

### Basic Kit vs. Producer Kit

All the DMD-based Drummers (using the Drum Kit Designer Plugin) and the Percussion-based Drummers (using the EXS24 Plugin) have two versions of their Drum Kits. That means each Drummer Patch exists twice, one creating a Basic Kit with a single Channel Strip (like a stereo mix of the the drum set) and the other one with the same name and a + sign at the end, creating a so-called Producer Kit that loads multiple Channel Strips, where each Drum Kit Piece is routed to its own Channel Strip, providing a professional mix environment.

To switch to the specific version of a Kit, you had to select the specific Patch in the Library Browser. The Producer Kits are located in their separate subfolder.

 ***10.3.2***

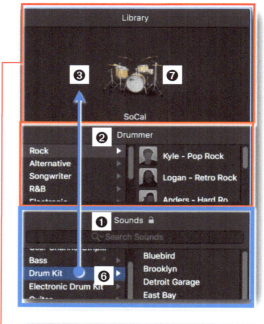

Now in version 10.3.2, there is a more elegant way to switch between the two Drum Kits. To use that new feature, you have to understand how the new interface of the Library Browser works, which I explained in great details in the first chapter.

### Icon Area - Drummer Area - Sounds Area

The Library Browser has three areas when a Drummer Track is selected. The Sounds Area ❶ at the bottom displays the Patches, the Drummer Area ❷ in the middle displays the available Drummers, and the Icon Area ❸ on top displays the icon and some details about what is selected in the Drummer Area or the Sounds Area.

- ▶ **Drummer Area**: If you *click* on the left column ❹ in the Drummer Area (i.e. "*Rock*"), then the Icon Area displays the current Drummer Card ❺.

- ▶ **Sounds Area**: If you *click* on the column displaying the "*Drum Kit*" ❻ category (or the "*Percussion*" category), it switches the Icon Area to show the icon of the currently selected Patch ❼. And here is the important part:

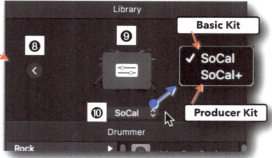

When you move the mouse cursor over that Icon Area when it shows the icon for the Drummer Patch, three things will change: The left-right arrows ❽ let you step through the Patches, the icon is covered by the Plugin Button ❾ (*click* to open the Plugin Window), and the third element is the little Menu Selector ❿ underneath. It shows the name of the currently selected Patch and when you *click* on it, a popup shows the Patches for the Basic Kit (i.e. *SoCal*) and the Producer Kit (*SoCal+*) of the currently selected Drummer, so you can easily switch between those two Patches without affecting the Drummer Regions on that Drummer Track.

# New Drum Machine Designer (DMD) Behavior

The behavior, when loading a Drum Machine Designer (DMD) Plugin from the Plugin Menu or loading any DMD-based Patch from the Library Browser, has slightly changed. Remember, the Drum Machine Designer "Plugin" is not really a Plugin. It loads a special Summing Stack (I call it a DMD Summing Stack) that has an instance of the Ultrabeat Plugin loaded.

 **10.3.1**

Logic tried to hide the complexity of the DMD-based "Plugin" by only creating a single Track ❶ (in this example "Big Room") when used on an Instrument Track or Drummer Track. The user doesn't even have to know that this is the Main Track of a very special Summing Stack (the DMD Summing Stack). Only if you open the Mixer, you will see the little triangle ❷ that indicate that this might be a Track Stack. When you *click* on it, you see the 34 Subtracks ❸.

When you needed a separate Track ❹ for one of the individual Drum Kit Pieces, you *ctr+click* on the corresponding Cell ❺ on the Drum Machine Designer Window and select "Create Track" ❻ from the Shortcut Menu. Or you can use the *Create Track* command (Key Command *ctr+T*) on a selected Channel Strip to create corresponding Track for that Channel Strip.

**10.3.2**

Now when you create a DMD-based Track, Logic creates the proper Summing Stack with the Main Track showing the disclosure triangle ❼. When you *click* on it, it expands, displaying all the 29 Subtracks ❽ assigned to the Channel Strips of the individual Ultrabeat outputs, so you don't have to create them separately ❻. The Create Track command now is obsolete, unless you deleted a Subtrack and wanted to re-create it.

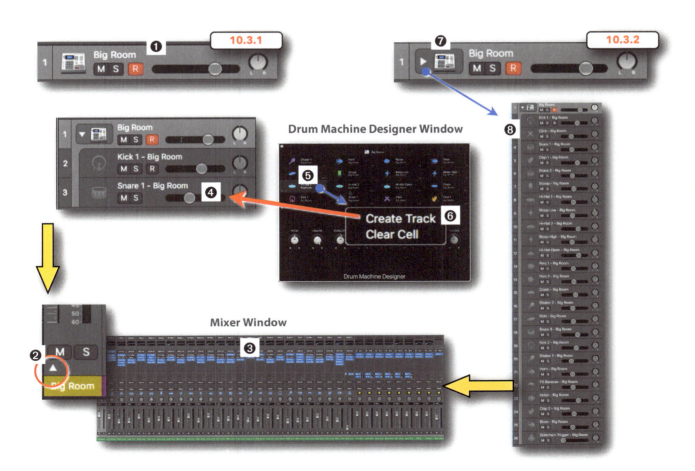

## Channel EQ

### All EQ Handles are visible when hovering over the EQ Display

Now when you move your mouse cursor over the EQ Display of the Channel EQ Plugin Window ❶, all EQ Handles ❷ (the dots along the frequency curve) become visible, instead of just the one you are moving over.

Channel EQ Plugin Window

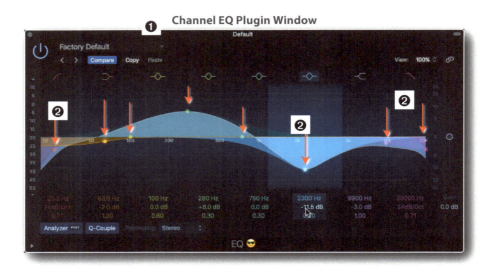

## Arpeggiator

Arpeggiator MIDI Plugin

### Adjust the Length of individual Step

In the *MIDI FX* "Arpeggiator", you can now *drag* the right border of a Step ❸ to freely adjust its length without being limited to the horizontal grid. That means that the Arpeggiator almost becomes a Sequencer by its own.

## Additional fourth Modulation Slider

*Clicking* on the "Settings" Button ❶ in the lower-right corner of the Retro Synth to reveal the Controllers. 10.3 had three controllers and 10.3.2 ❷ now has added a fourth controller ❸ with a Modulation Slider and the Target.

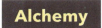

# New Browser Column Options

The Browser View ❸ in Alchemy has two more Column Options, "**Newer Than**" and "**Older Than**" ❷.

Alchemy Plugin Window

# New Options for in the Note Properties Menu

Select the Advanced Tab ❸ and in the Modulation Rack *click* on the Modulation Selector ❹. The *Note Property* submenu ❺ has three new options ❻, *Stepped4*, *Stepped8,* and *Stepped16*. They function like the *Flip Flop* option, but also produce a modulation signal that cycles through equally spaced values between successive notes.

## New Synthesized Formant Filter Shapes

The popup menu ❶ for selecting the synthesized formant filter ❷ is rearranged with submenus ❸ containing new synthesized formant filter shapes with more aggressive *Parallel* ❹, *Comb* ❺, and *Vowel Bright* ❻ shapes.

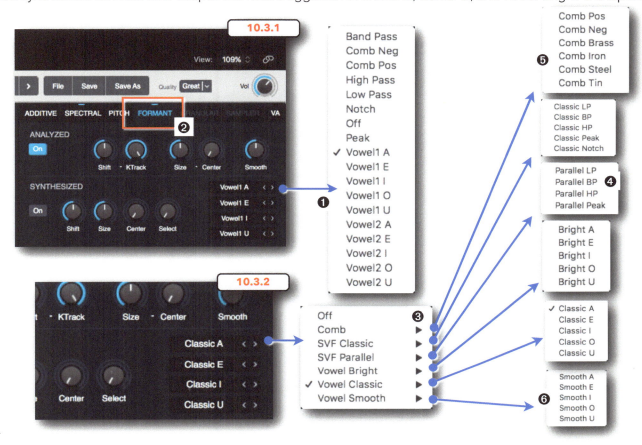

## A new "Tune Control" in the Noise Section

Select the Advanced Tab ❼, *click* on a Source Button ❽ on the left (A, B, C, or D) and select the VA Button (Virtual Analog) ❾ in the upper-right corner. The Noise Section below now has an additional knob, the Tune Control ❿ (-48 semitones ... +48 semitones).

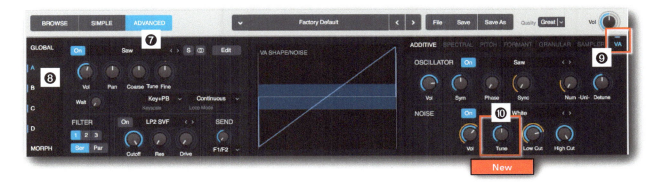

# New Additive Effects

There is a total of seven new Additive Effects ❶ in the three popup menus ❷ (*Saw+Noise, Noise, Comb, EQ, Filter, Strum, Ripples*) plus additional controls for *Pulse/Saw*.

# Effects are organized in Categories

The 17 Effects ❸ have been rearranged into categories and their submenus ❹.

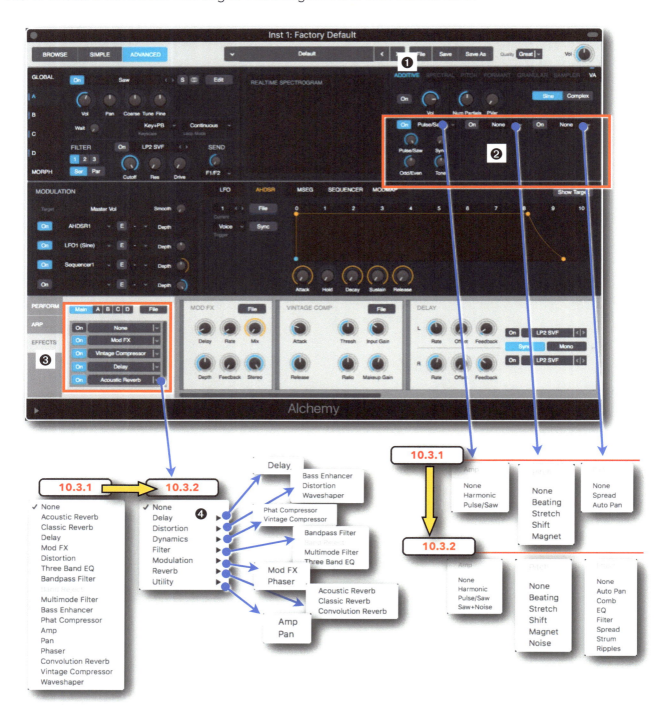

6 - Mixer & Plugins

## New Default Rate for the Arpeggiator is 1/16

Select the Browser or Advanced Tab and click the ARP Tab ❶ in the lower-left corner to make the Arpeggiator section visible. The Rate Control ❷ is now set to 1/16 as a default for a new instance of the Arpeggiator. It was 1/8 before.

## New Key Trigger "Cycle Reset"

Select the Browser or Advanced Tab and click the ARP Tab ❶ in the lower-left corner to make the Arpeggiator section visible. The Key Trigger Menu ❸ now has a new option *"Cycle Reset"* ❹ that insures the pattern always starts at the first note at step 1 of the sequencer.

## 21 New Arpeggiator Presets

The File Selector ❺ in the ARP section opens a menu with the Preset Submenu ❻ that contains 21 new Arpeggiator Presets ❼.

## Default Auto Gain in Morph XY/Lin is off

Select the Advanced Tab, *click* the Morph Tab ❽ on the left below the Sound Sources, and select the Morph XY or the Morph Lin ❾ on the far right. The Auto Gain Button ❿ in this section is set to off now by default.

# Default Keyswitch is now "KEYSW1"

Select the Advanced Tab ❶, *click* on Source Button ❷ on the left (A, B, C, or D), and *click* the Edit Button ❸ to switch to the Source Edit Window ❹. When selecting the *Keyswitch* ❺ option in the Group Rules Menu on the left, the default option will now be *KEYSW1* ❻ instead of *SNAP1*.

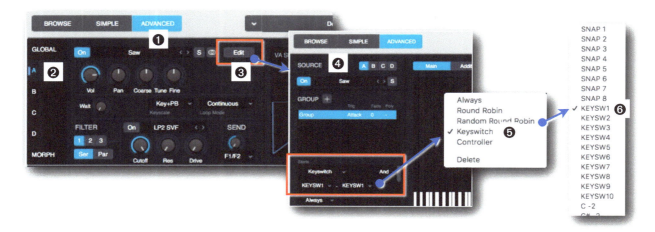

# Other Alchemy Improvements

And here are a few more of the improvements and changes in Alchemy:

- ☑ Alchemy uses up to 40% less memory than previous versions.
- ☑ The maximum number of partials in Alchemy's Great quality mode has been raised from 128 to 256.
- ☑ When importing EXS instruments, Alchemy now merges EXS groups that are mapped to the same keyswitch or articulation.
- ☑ The browser in Alchemy now retains user choices for column selections when switching from one preset to another.
- ☑ Alchemy includes an automatic time align feature for improved morphing.
- ☑ Copy/pasted modulations now include the full routings assigned to all associated depth knobs.
- ☑ It is now possible to modulate Alchemy's Keyswitch knob with Arp Mod.
- ☑ Alchemy's Additive Effects knobs for Pulse/Saw - Sync, Shift - Pitch and Magnet - Pitch now show semitones when being edited.
- ☑ Alchemy's modulators now have a new On trigger mode, which allows Effects parameters to be re-triggered on all new MIDI notes.
- ☑ Alchemy's Additive Effects knobs for Pulse/Saw - Sync, Shift - Pitch and Magnet - Pitch now show semitones when being edited.

## More Flat Design

### Updated Project Chooser Dialog

The Project Chooser Dialog, the window that opens when you use the Main Menu command **File ➤ New from Template...** (Key Command **cmd+N**) got a little bit of a makeover to be in line with the rest of Logic's flat design. Also, a few other things changed:

☑ New flat icons ❶: Love it or hate it, that's how Apple rolls nowadays.

☑ New Template "**Music for Picture**"❷: This is a new Template with all the instruments loaded, so you can start scoring your kid's Birthday Party or your next Star Wars movie.

☑ The *Empty Project* Template is listed first ❸: The *Empty Project* Template is now listed as the first Template instead of the last ❹ on the window

☑ New Windows Title "**Choose a Project**" ❺: The window title is now "*Choose a Project*" instead of "*Logic Pro X*".

**Project Chooser Dialog**

BTW, the additional folders in the sidebar ❻ of this screenshot are custom folders inside the *My Template* folder (**~/Music/Audio Music Apps/Project Templates/**) that you can create to organize your own Templates better. More of those tips, like creating your own Template icons, are in my book "Logic Pro X - Tips, Tricks, Secrets #2".

# New Track Dialog

 **Recap**

The New Tracks Dialog (*click* on the New Tracks Button ➕ , Main Menu *Track ➤ New Tracks...* or Key Command *opt+cmd+N*) can be displayed as a big window with icons ❶ or as a smaller window ❷ just with text buttons. You can select which display you prefer with the checkbox "*Chose icons in New Tracks dialog*" ❸ in the *Preferences ➤ Display ➤ General ➤ Windows*.

**10.3.2**

The New Tracks Dialog with icons now also has new flat graphics ❹, plus new text ❺ that better describes the available options.

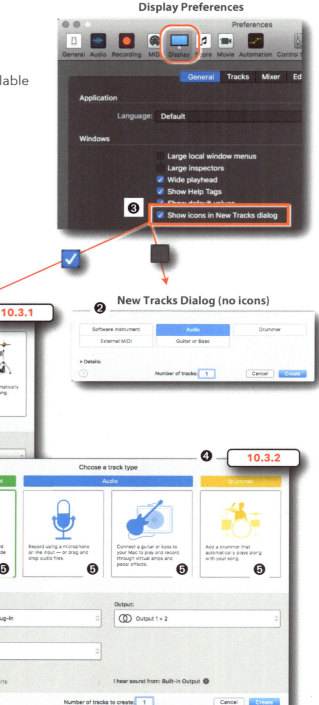

**Display Preferences**

**❶ New Tracks Dialog (with icons)**

**10.3.1**

**❷ New Tracks Dialog (no icons)**

**10.3.2**

You can use the Touch Bar even without a recent MacBook Pro, just install the app Touché. I explain all the functionality of the Touch Bar in great detail in my book "Logic Pro X - What' New in 10.3"

## Key Command access from any View

Pressing any Modifier Keys will automatically switch the Touch Bar to Key Commands View, displaying those assigned Key Commands, regardless of the current Main View. Tapping a key command on the Touch Bar when the Key Commands window is open now selects the command in the window.

## More Images for Key Commands

Logic now has images ❶ for more Key Commands. Much better than those cryptic text labels ❷.

## Two Lines for Long Key Command Name

If the custom "*Short Name*" ❸ for a Key Command is too long to fit on the button ❹, it now switches to two lines with a smaller 11pt font ❺.

## Two Lines for Long Smart Controls Names

If the name for a Smart Control is too long ❻ to fit on the Touch Bar button, it now switches to two lines with a smaller 11pt font ❼.

## Environment

It is assuring that the Environment Window (*cmd+0*) still gets some attention from the Logic team, which is assuring for all Logic power users who still live and breath "Environment".

### Environment Window again has a Link Button

The Link Button ❶ has returned, the purple "Same Level Link Button" to be specific.

### Opt+click to Clear All Monitor Objects

The Monitor Object ❷ in the Environment (Local Menu *New ➤ Monitor*) is handy display component that shows all the MIDI Events and Fader Events that passing through a MIDI connection.

*Clicking* on a Monitor Object clears the display of all the MIDI Events. Now when *opt+clicking* ❸ on a Monitor Object clears the display of all ❹ the Monitor Objects on that window, which comes in handy if you have a complex Environment configuration with lots of Monitor Objects.

**Environment Window**

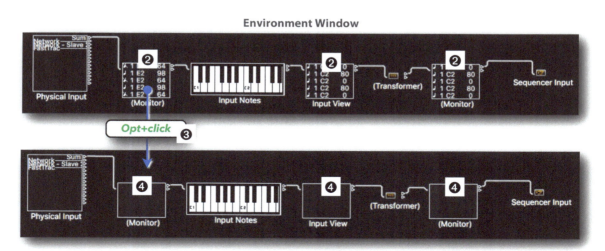

# MIDI Transformer with Note Scale Parameter

###  Piano Roll

The Piano Roll Editor has a feature in the Local Inspector called "Scale Quantize" ❶. Instead of quantizing the selected Notes to a "timing grid", it lets you quantize (transpose) the notes to a "pitch grid" in the form of musical scales (major, minor, pentatonic, etc. that you select from a popup menu.

**Piano Roll Editor**

###  Transformer Object

This Scale Quantize feature has been added to the Transformer Object ❷ in the Environment Window. When placed between the Physical Input Object and the Sequencer Object, you can restrict your life playing from your MIDI keyboard to a specific scale, avoiding that you play "wrong" notes. Think about autotune for you lesser-skilled keyboard players.

▶ Create a Transformer Object (*New* ➤ *Transformer*) in the Environment and place it in the MIDI signal flow ❷.

▶ *Double-click* the Transformer Object to open the Transformer Window ❸.

▶ Select "*Use Map*" ❹ from the Pitch Operator.

▶ 10.3.2 has added a new selector button in the lower right corner "Note Quantize" ❺.

▶ *Click* on the button, and the same menu ❻ from the Scale Quantize feature opens where you select a specific key and a scale.

**Environment Window**

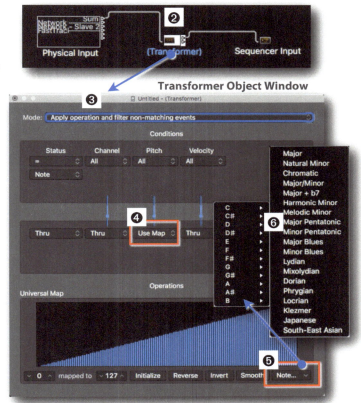

### Transformer Window

That new Note Scale Selector is also added to the MIDI Transform Window ❼ (*cmd+9*). Here you have to select the *Transposition* Preset ❽ first.

The functionality of the window is otherwise identical to the Transformer Object; the only difference is that here, you apply the command to selected MIDI Events, similar to the Scale Quantize feature in the Piano Roll Editor.

**MIDI Transform Window** ❼

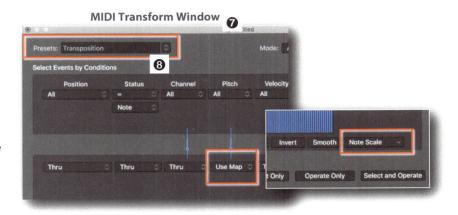

## New Yellow Quick Help Popovers

Logic's Quick Help feature got a new useful variation. The result might be a bit confusing because now there are different combinations for what is displayed and how. This is a typical example where Logic sometimes provides too many options that might leave the user confused. My advice is to try to understand the available options and only use the ones that fit your workflow. Ignore the others until you change your workflow.

You can toggle the Quick Help feature in three ways:

- *Click* the Quick Help Button ❶  on the Control Bar
- Main Menu *Help* ➤ *Quick Help*
- Key Command *sh+/* ❸

**Control Bar: Quick Help Button**

**Main Menu: Help**

**Key Commands**

Now let's look at the different combinations:

### 🌑 *Quick Help Off*

If Quick Help is disabled, then a yellow popover ❹ appears when you move the mouse over the Quick Help Button ⑦ on the Control Bar, explaining what happens when you click the button (enable Quick Help).

### 🌑 *Quick Help On (Inspector)*

If Quick Help is enabled ⑦ and the Main Inspector is visible in the Main Window, then the Quick Help Area ❺ is displayed on top of the Main Inspector, displaying any explanation about any control or area you currently move your mouse cursor over.

If you haven't tried it yet; it is quite handy to get around in Logic (especially if you are new to Logic). Those "hotspots" that trigger a popover also work for virtually all the FX Plugins and Software Instrument Plugins where you have tons of knobs and buttons. Just move over any control and Logic tells you what it does and what it is used for. Very powerful.

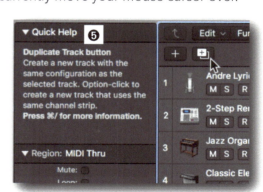

## 🔆 Quick Help On (Floating Window)

This is a variation to display the Quick Help Area as a separate floating window ❶ instead of in the Main Inspector. You can achieve that in two ways

▶ *Drag* the header of the Quick Help Area in the Inspector away and it tears off as a separate window.

▶ If the Main Inspector is closed and you enabled Quick Help, it automatically opens as a floating window.

### *Attention*

Enabling Quick Help now has an additional function in 10.3.2.

When you move the mouse cursor over the Quick Help Button ❷ ⦿ on the Control Bar, yellow popovers will appear over the main areas of the Logic window that currently has key focus. This could be any other window besides the Main Window.

## 🔆 Quick Help On + Quick Help Follows Pointer

10.3.2 has a new command in the Main Menu *Help ➤ Quick Help Follows Pointer* ❸ (also available as Key Command), that disables the Quick Help Area in the Inspector (or the floating window) and displays a yellow Quick Help Popover ❹ directly where you move the cursor at. This way, the information about a control or an area is right there without taking your eyes off and looking at the separate Quick Help Area.

Move your mouse around, and the yellow Quick Help Popover appears everywhere on the window where there is a hotspot with information. This is quite annoying during regular operation, but extremely helpful when learning or reviewing controls and functionality in Logic (especially with Plugin).

### *Tip*

When a Quick Help window is open, don't forget that you can use the Key command *cmd+/* which opens the "Logic Pro Help" window, a system-wide help mechanism (not to be confused with a popular website).

I discuss all the various help features in the Workflow chapter of my book "Logic Pro X - The Details", especially how to use the built-in "Smart Help" mechanism, your personal online tutor at your finger tips.

# Window Header of Transport Float is renamed to "Transport"

 ***Recap***

The so-called Transport Float ❶ is a floating window with the main controls of the Control Bar. Not only can you configure the controls differently than on the Control Bar, but you can also open multiple Transport Floats to really customize your screen real estate.

 ***10.3.2***

The earth-shattering improvement in 10.3.2 is that the window title of the Transport Float was renamed from "*Control Bar*" to "*Transport*" ❷. As you can see, the Logic Developer Team is hard at work, paying attention to the smallest details.

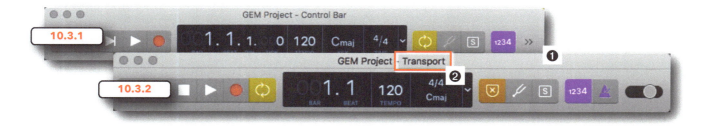

# Window Header has changed from "Strip Silence" to "Remove Silence"

The "*Strip Silence*" ❸ command has been renamed to "***Remove Silence***". You can see that name change on the Remove Silence Dialog ❹, The Remove Silence Button ❺ on the Main Window's Toolbar and the command in the Shortcut Menu *Split ➤ Remove Silence from Audio Region...* ❻ when you ***ctr+click*** on an Audio Region.

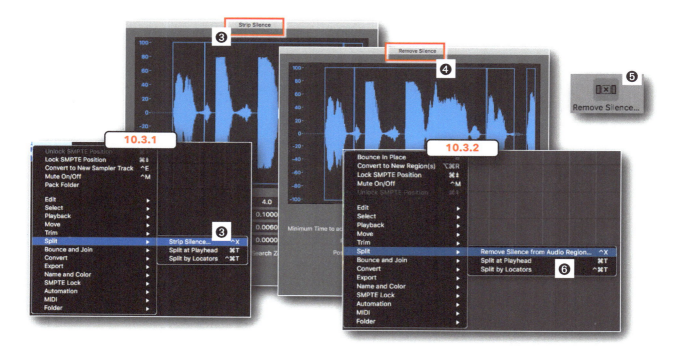

## "Do not show this message again" checkbox in Add Tempo Dialog

 **10.3.1**

When you import an audio file that contains tempo information, you get an Alert Dialog ❷ asking if you want to import those Tempo Events into your Tempo Track or not. If you import a lot of audio files, then this Alert Dialog becomes quite annoying.

 **10.3.2**

Now the Alert Dialog has a checkbox ❸ like many other alters that lets you dismiss that specific dialog for the future.

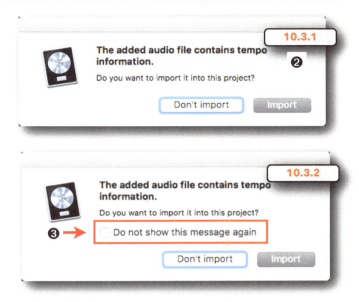

## "Don't show again" checkbox in Aux Import Dialog

When you are in the All Files Browser ❹ to import individual Channel Strips that include Aux Channel Strips, the Aux Import Dialog ❺ pops up, asking if you want to create new Aux Channel Strips or want to choose existing Aux Channel Strip. With a lot of Aux Channel Strips to import, this dialog can get annoying. Now you also have a checkbox "Don't show again" ❻ to dismiss this dialog.

Remember, the "Reset Warnings" Button ❼ in the *Preferences ➤ General ➤ Notifications* lets you reset those alerts, so they will show up again.

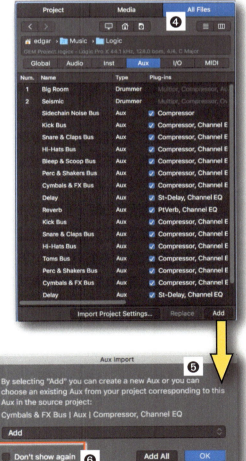

**General Preferences**

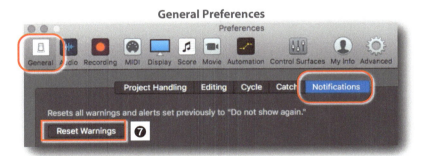

# Disconnect/Reconnect Split Stereo Files

 **Recap**

Split Stereo Files are two mono audio files with the same file name and the file extension .L and .R, indicating that both files belong to a stereo signal, with one file containing the left channel and the other file containing the right channel. This was the standard when early DAWs could only process mono files. DAWs nowadays can process interleaved audio files (one file containing multiple channels) and display them as a single Audio Region. Logic pretty much abandoned Split Stereo Files to a point, where you cannot import Split Stereo Files anymore because they are automatically "combined" into an interleaved stereo file, represented by a single Audio Region.

 **10.3.2**

10.3.2 brings back some previous functionality for the Split Stereo Files. When you open an old Logic Project that had Split Stereo Files, you can spot them by their special split stereo icon ⬤⬤ ❶ instead of a mono icon ⬤ or stereo interleaved icon ⬤.

A few things to pay attention to:

▸ Editing (truncating, renaming, etc.) one of the Split Stereo Files (.L ❷) will edit the other one (.R ❸) the same way.

▸ The Local Edit Menu in the Project Audio Window now displays the old command "*Disconnect Selected Stereo Files*" ❹ (from the Logic Pro 9 days) that lets you disconnect those Split Stereo Files to treat them separately.

▸ Once files are disconnected, the icon changes to a mono symbol ⬤ ❺ and the command in the Edit Menu changes to "*Reconnect All Split Stereo Files*" ❻.

▸ Using the "Reconnect All Split Stereo Files" command connects the Split Stereo Files again to their previous state ⬤⬤ ❶.

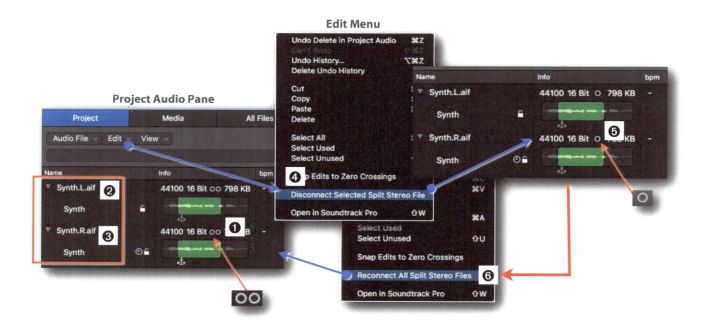

# Final Cut Pro XML imports Parent Roles as Folder Stacks

This new feature is a major improvement for exchanging Projects between Final Cut Pro X and Logic Pro X using the "Final Cut Pro XML" protocol. (***File ➤ Import ➤ Final Cut Pro XML...***).

The recent Final Cut Pro X 10.3 update (if you want to learn that fine piece of software, I have you covered with the perfect book "Final Cut Pro X 10.3 - How It Works") introduced a major improvement to Roles ❶ and Subroles ❷ that are similar in their functionality to Summing Stacks in Logic. Here is how Logic takes advantage of that:

**Final Cut Pro X (10.3.3)**

 ***10.3.1***

In 10.3.1, when you import a FCPx Project, all the Audio Clips are imported as Audio Regions placed across as many Audio Tracks ❸ as needed, loosing the structure and organization of the FCPx Roles and Subroles.

 ***10.3.2***

Now for each Parent Role ❶, Logic creates a Summing Stack ❹ (named after that Parent Role) and puts all Audio Clip assigned to a specific Subroles ❷ inside those corresponding Summing Stacks on corresponding Tracks ❺. I cheated on the screenshot by adding the colors manually, because the color assignment from FCPx, unfortunately, is not transferred to the Logic Project (yet?).

Large Final Cut Pro X Projects now also load much quicker.

## Music XML Export to Dorico

There are two improvements when exporting a Score via the MusicXML protocol (Main Menu *File ➤ Export ➤ Score as MusicXML...*)

Main Menu File ➤ Export ➤

▶  The MusicXML files are now more compatible with Dorico

▶  The MusicXML files now include TAB Staff Styles

## Logic Remote Improvements

▶  The labels for the buttons that halve and double the delay length in the Stereo Delay plug-in are now labeled correctly in Logic Remote.

▶  The Sync Time control in the Tape Delay plug-in is now visible in Logic Remote.

▶  Logic Remote now immediately updates the Track display in the Mixer and LCD after the track order is changed in Logic Pro.

▶  Logic Remote now reliably displays all plug-in parameters.

There are a few new items, new tabs, and some items that have been moved around in the Preferences.

**General ➤ Editing**

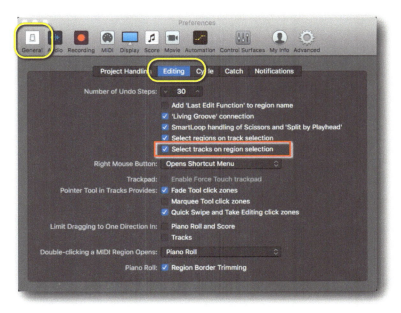

▶ **New**:
"Select tracks on region selection"

When this checkbox is enabled, selecting any Region on a Track Lane in the Workspace will automatically select the Track that corresponding Track.

**Audio ➤ General**

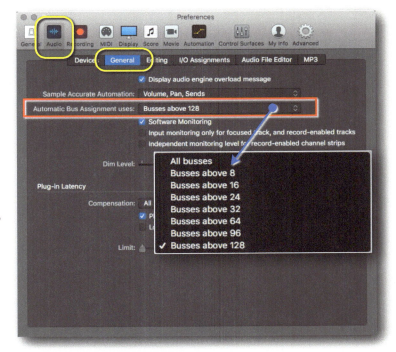

▶ **New**:
"Automatic Bus Assignment uses"

Some Patches automatically use busses for their routing assignments, especially the Patches based on the Drum Machine Designer. Selecting any option from the popup menu forces Logic to use busses with higher Bus numbers, so they are easier to manage with the busses that you assign manually, most likely in the lower range.

 **Recording**

▶ **New**:
"Recording Project Settings..."

Some Preferences windows have a button that
lets you open the corresponding Project
Settings window. This new addition to the
Recording Preferences does exactly that. It
opens the Recording Project Settings window.

 **Display ➤ Tracks**

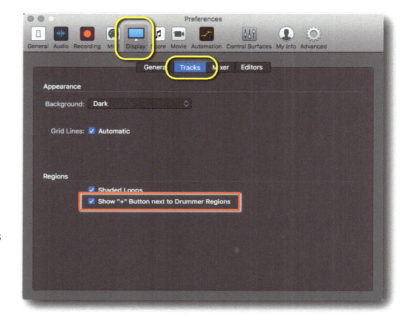

▶ **New**:
Show "+" Button next to Drummer
Region

Enable this checkbox to show the yellow +
button ⊕ next to a Drummer Region that lets
you add a new 8-bar Drummer Region or fill
the gap with a Drummer Region if the space is
less than 8 bars.

 **Display ➤ Mixer**

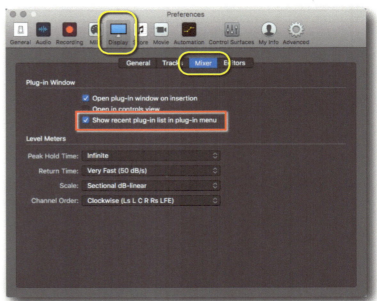

▶ **New**:
Show recent plug-in list in plug-in menu

If enabled, the Audio FX Plugin Menu and the Software Instrument Plugin Menu show the last five Plugins that you loaded.

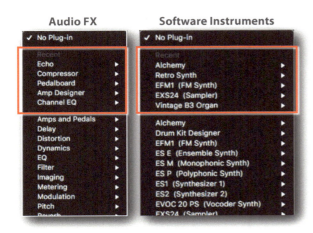

## Project Settings

There doesn't seem to be any changes this time in the Project Settings.

## Main Menu

I'm sure there are more changes in various menus, but I found only the following ones.

In the Main Menu **Mix ➤ Create Track Automation ➤**, the command "Fade Out" has been renamed to "*Create Volume Fade Out on Main Output*". And the Trim submenu in the Edit Menu now includes the commands "*Region Start to Previous Region*" and "*Region End to Next Region*".

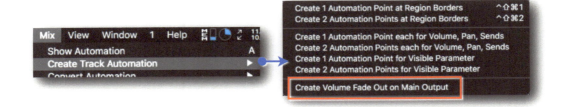

## New - Renamed

There are only a few Key Commands addition and changes:

### ➡ New Key Commands

 **Global Commands**

- Quick Help Follows Pointer
- Show/Hide Help Tags

**Main Window Tracks**

- Remove Fades

- Show/Hide All Inactive Track Alternatives

- Copy Section Between Locators (Global)

### ➡ Renamed Key Commands

**Main Window Tracks**

- Create Volume Fade Out on Main Output [was "Create Fade Out"]

- Remove Silence from Audio Region... (*ctr+X*) [was "Strip Silence"]

# Conclusion

This concludes my manual *"Logic Pro X - What's New in 10.3.2"*.

If you find my visual approach of explaining features and concepts helpful, please recommend my books to others or maybe write a review on Amazon or the iBooks Store. This will help me to continue this series.
To check out other books in my "Graphically Enhanced Manuals" series, go to my website at:
www.DingDingMusic.com/Manuals

To contact me directly, email me at: GEM@DingDingMusic.com

More information about my day job as a composer and links to my social network sites are on my website:
www.DingDingMusic.com

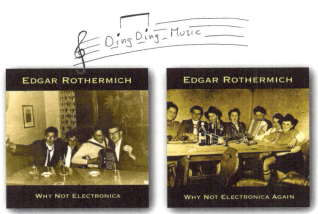

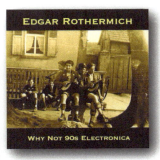

Listen to my music on SoundCloud

Thanks for your interest and your support,

*Edgar Rothermich*

Conclusion

99